How to Ma
Like You

*19 Science-Based Methods to Increase Your
Charisma, Spark Attraction, Win Friends, and
Connect Effortlessly*

By reading this document, the reader agrees that under no circumstances is the author responsible for any losses, direct or indirect, which are incurred as a result of the use of information contained within this document, including, but not limited to, — errors, omissions, or inaccuracies.

Table of Contents

Your Free Gift

As a way of saying thanks for your purchase, I'm offering the book ***Bulletproof Confidence Checklist*** for FREE to my readers.

To get instant access just go to:

https://theartofmastery.com/confidence/

Inside the book, you will discover:

- Why we develop shyness & social anxiety
- Powerful strategies for overcoming social anxiety
- Become more confident by destroying these negative traits
- How to easily prevent the "awkward silence" in a conversation

- Confidence checklist to ensure you're on the right path of self-development

Introduction

"Confidence is the most beautiful thing you can possess." –
Sabrina Carpenter

Imagine being back in your school days. Take a moment to remember what it was like. I'm talking around the age of 13 or 14, just heading into your teenage years.

You come and go from school. You sit in lessons and play games during break time. You work on group projects with classmates and study for your essays and exams. You meet your first love, your first girlfriend or boyfriend, and run around on weekends with your friends.

As you grew up, you started to settle into your friend groups. You may have stayed friends with the people from your childhood, or as you moved into higher education, college, and university, you started mixing with new groups of friends. People came, and people went. As you learned more about yourself and what you liked and didn't like, you started meeting new people who liked the same things.

Whether you loved going out and partying, reading, hanging out, watching movies, playing video games, or loved sports, there were always people around you who you would call your friends. Maybe you're still friends with some of those people now, or perhaps you've gone off in different directions in life.

Over the last few years, I've been thinking about this journey of friendships that we all go through. I know some childhoods aren't great. Kids can be mean, and there are things like bullying that can leave some of them feeling a bit like an outcast. But even then, I remember kids in my school who were picked on by some of the other kids, but they still had a group of friends to call their own.

My ailment was my social anxiety. It wasn't too bad in school, but it started to kick in when I headed into my teenage years and then college. I just found that I couldn't speak to anyone and make new relationships. I had a few friends that I went to school with and stayed in touch with them now and then, but it was so difficult to meet and connect with new people.

I just couldn't seem to do it.

My self-esteem was through the floor, and this battered my confidence in myself. It felt like I was stuck in this vicious cycle of not being able to talk to people, feeling anxious about it, and then that further propelling the feelings of not being able to talk to others. It was holding my life back.

It got to a point during my 20s when I landed my first "real" job in sales and marketing when I started to realize that this was a problem that was holding me back. The fact you're reading this book right now means you probably already know what I'm talking about.

That feeling of looking back to your childhood years and wondering how you made friends so easily and how it was possible to talk to people without being shy or overthinking every interaction. That feeling of wonderment of how you could have so many friends and acquaintances when you were younger, but now you have a handful of friends, some of which you only speak to once in a blue moon.

Don't worry; you're not alone in this way of thinking.

The New Age of Connection

We all live in the new, unprecedented hyper-connected world that is the modern human era. Things like social media have taken over and become an absolute cornerstone in our everyday lives. Human connection is going through a shift that has never happened before in the history of the human race.

Statistics from 2019 found that 61% of Americans admit to having regular feelings of loneliness, up 7% on the year before, and that 52% feel lonely "most of the time" or "always." A similar YouGov poll in 2019 found that 21% of Americans have "no close friends," and 58% sometimes or always feel as though nobody knows them that well. As you can probably guess from these stats, it comes as no surprise that 53% of people find it difficult to make friends.

These statistics are mirrored globally in nearly all Western countries, including most of the EU, the United Kingdom, Mexico, Japan, Greece, Israel, and many more. This isn't just something happening in small pockets of the world; it's happening all over it.

These are many revelationary statistics, some of which probably surprise you, but they paint a clear picture. We are all becoming more disconnected from one another, and the more this disconnect continues, the harder it seems to become to reconnect again. When you chuck in the isolating nature of society, politics, gender, and race discussions, and not forgetting the massive impact of the 2020 COVID-19 pandemic, these are issues that are going to be causing more and more problems on a large scale.

But I don't want to talk about the large scale impact of this loneliness pandemic. It makes everything feel like there's too much doom and gloom, which is not the case. It may sound simple, but you've got to scale everything down and look at your relationships and ability to connect in your own life. You've got to focus on the small, personal scale.

Once you're here, you can start learning about how your mind works and what's happening within you to make you disconnect from others or discover why you're finding it hard to connect with new people. You can then take this information as a foundation to learn new techniques on how to nurture vibrant and exciting relationships and new skills on how to meet and talk to new people, even total strangers.

You give yourself the chance to build new friendships and then build them into friendships that can last for years to come. You learn how to reconnect, and this is exactly what we're going to be focusing on throughout this book.

A New Day. A New Beginning.

Riddled with social anxiety, I spent most of my early and mid-twenties in a rut. I was an outcast and felt lonely pretty much every day. I was that guy in the background at work that you probably knew my name or saw at the Christmas party once or twice, but you can't even remember having a conversation with. My cheeks are going red and hot just thinking about it.

It got to the point when I was about 28 when I thought, *Enough is enough. There must be a better way of living. I must be able to learn how to talk to people.* I remember one day there was a promotion coming up for a manager job in my sales firm. I was the lead project manager for a new client we were taking on, and it was one of those opportunities that fitted me perfectly. I knew that if I got the job, I would be so good at it. It would be my chance to shine. Unfortunately, I never dared to speak up, and even in my interview, my boss said I was good, but I just wasn't the people person they were looking for.

Do you know who did get the job?

The confident, charismatic guy that everyone loved, greeted when he walked into the office, and even the postman who came in would stop to chat with him. God, I used to be so envious of the way he was. It wasn't even arrogant or egotistic. It was natural charm and charisma that drew you in. He was genuine, and even if you had nothing in common interest-wise, you still wanted to chat with him and hear what he had to say.

I'm not a massive believer in auras and spiritual connection, but there's no doubt that he was one of those guys who walked into a room, and everyone felt his presence. I'm sure you know people in your life who are the same.

It took a few years and still a lot of practice to this day, and I found out that you can become like this person, but not exactly this person. You can become your *own* person. You can become the true, unadulterated, unfiltered, genuine, connection-worthy you. As with everything in life, all it takes is a little know-how, practice, and willingness to open your mind to what is possible.

Permit yourself right here and now to open your mind to this new way of being.

If you can't, then take that last sentence as me giving you permission to open your mind. Throughout the following pages of this book, I'm going to detail everything I've learned on my journey so you can increase your charisma, spark attraction among the people in your life, win friends, nurture and build relationships, attract romantic partners, and connect with other human beings in a way you've never connected with them before.

After a lot of work on myself, I've narrowed everything down to just 19 easy-to-follow methods, backed up by scientific research, and complete with everything you need to know about how to make friends in the modern age. Every single method here is actionable right here, right now, and by the time you're done reading this book, you're going to feel good about yourself in a way you wouldn't even believe.

And with that, I'm sure you've heard enough from me, and you're excited to get into it, so follow me down the rabbit hole, keep hands and feet inside the carriage at all times, and let's get learning.

Part One – The Start of Something New

"Strangers are just friends waiting to happen." – Rod Mckuen

Every single relationship that has, does, or will ever exist always starts the same, and that same way is one person talking to another person. In order to create a relationship, you need to meet people and start that initial connection.

It doesn't matter what kind of relationships you want in your life, or the kinds of relationships you're reading this book to try and attract. First impressions are always the most important impressions, and you need to have the ability to talk to new people, make them like you from the word go, and even have the confidence to make this all happen in the first place.

This is why I'm going to start here. Throughout the following chapters (which I'm going to be titling as methods), we're going to explore some of the best ways you have the confidence to meet and talk to new people, get the conversations flowing, and basically get your foot in the door when it comes to connecting with other people.

Method 1 – It's About the Smile

"When you're smiling, the whole world smiles with you." –
Louis Armstrong

When Louis Armstrong, one of the most popular jazz artists in history, sang these words for the first time, he probably never imagined that scientific studies would someday back up his claim. You probably know this already and have experienced it countless times throughout your life, which is why this is my first and foremost method for nurturing beautiful relationships with other people. It literally revolves around one action.

Smiling.

Simply smiling is such a powerful action, both on a physical and subconscious level. Smiling is a known human trait throughout the world, meaning it doesn't matter what culture you're in or what people you're talking to; smiling makes us feel the same. It's human instinct that we react the way we do when we see someone smiling. Best of all, this has been proven repeatedly, both by personal experiences and scientific studies.

In 2002, a Swedish study researching body language, mimicry, and emotional empathy found that people who were subject to pictures of other people smiling found it "incredibly difficult" to frown or display traditionally negative emotions. They actually went further than this and found that doing anything other than smiling when you see somebody else smiling needs to have a conscious effort to do. That's how natural smiling is.

Of course, smiling is a very positive emotion and makes you feel positive feelings. When it comes to building relationships and friendships with other people, you want people to see you in a positive way, which is why smiling is such a powerful method for attracting other people. Think about when you see someone at work crying, looking sad, or looking extremely angry. What do you do?

Well, if you're like most people, or at least like me, you'll feel very uncertain about how you're going to proceed. Do you talk to them? Help them? Try and make them laugh? Leave them on their own for a bit? There's so much uncertainty with these kinds of emotions, and everyone who experiences them is left feeling very unsure.

On the other hand, if you go into work and someone smiles towards, nods their head, or is even just smiling at their computer, the situation feels stable and secure. You can talk to that person, and if anything, you feel like you want to speak to that person more, just because they're smiling. As you're reading this, I'm sure you're imagining situations in your life where this has happened, or at least you are now!

Think about a restaurant you went to where the waitress greeted you with a massive smile before showing you to your table and how welcomed that made you feel. Now compare that with the grunt the other restaurant waiter gave you who was clearly having a bad day and made you feel uncomfortable. I'm sure you understand what I'm saying.

Your Smile Changes How You See the World

And how others perceive the world.

A study published in "Social Cognitive and Affective Neuroscience" in 2015 had researchers who did some very interesting research on this topic. In their study, they found that the very act of smiling or seeing somebody else smile physically changes our emotions and feelings. They found this out by actively monitoring the electrical activity in the brains of their volunteers. The results?

When people smiled at the volunteers, this instantly made them feel more positive. They ran many tests, and as a benchmark to this research, they discovered that when human beings see what you would call a "neutral" face, you would automatically assume that person to be feeling neutral. I mean, are there any surprises there?

But, when you see someone smiling, you automatically take that as the person feeling "happy." When it comes to making new friends and connecting with people, this is such an important consideration to take on board. By smiling, you're sharing positive energy with the people around you. This makes them want to approach you, connect with you, and simply be around you more. Just walking into a room and smiling is a great way to initially start a conversation and get people interested in what you have to say.

Likewise, when you smile yourself, your brain releases feel-good chemicals, known as serotonin, that make you feel good. Don't believe me? Try it right now. Look away from the book and out of a window, towards someone you love, a pet, a stranger, a tree, or anything that happens to be around you. Now simply smile. Even if you don't feel like smiling, just try it.

I'll give you a second.

Even when I did this right now, as I write this, I can't help but push air out of my nose and have a little laugh to myself. That's the power that smiling can have. Even if you're having the worst day you can imagine, taking some time to smile and just be present is enough to invoke a positive mindset. And, as research has proven time and time again, this positive effect reaches out to the people around you.

Never underestimate the power of a smile.

Action Time: Smile More!

Since this is the first chapter, I will make the takeaway easy and something you can start working on right now. Consider this your homework, but you don't get a grade at the end of it. You instead get the opportunity to create more meaningful relationships and connect much more easily with people who come and go in your life.

Here's what you need to do.

Ready?

You just need to smile more!

Yes, that is it. I know it sounds simple, and you probably guessed that's what I was going to say anyway, but, and I'll say this one last time to drive home this message, you can never underestimate the power a smile can have.

Try it. When you next go into a shop, talk to the cashier, pass someone in the street, talk to someone at work, or see your partner when you get into the house. Smile at them. Say hi and beam your best smile in their direction. If you're introducing yourself to a new customer, make the conscious effort to smile at them, and make yourself as appealing as possible.

The results of doing this speak for themselves, so try it and become your own proof. Now, I know this method is really simple, and you've probably heard something like this before, but you'll be amazed by how few people know how powerful this is. If you really can't bring yourself to smile, then you could always think about getting a dog.

Dogs always make people smile.

Anyway, all jokes aside, smiling more isn't the only approach to winning friends and becoming more approachable. This is just the tip of the iceberg. Let's get into some other approaches that can help you achieve your connection goals.

Method 2 – Always Make the First Move

"You can't stay in your corner of the Forest waiting for others to come to you. You have to go to them sometimes."
– A. Milne, Winnie-the-Pooh

Imagine this.

You could get onto a bus or a train, and the person sitting next to you may be someone you were destined to be best friends with. You may have so much in common: the same interests, the same music tastes, and the same love of classic movies. It's effortless that you two would share many great experiences and could spend an entire lifetime having fun, making memories, and enjoying life in so many amazing ways.

However, there's a catch. One of you has to speak to the other first.

It's heartbreaking to me that we live in such a closed-off and secluded world, isolating ourselves from one another. Hey, I've been on both sides. I've been the closed-off person who sits on the train and does everything I can to avoid acknowledging existence from everyone else around me. I've also been the guy who's sat and watched everyone else around me be that person.

We live in a world where we're afraid to talk to each other. Heck, we're afraid to look each other in the eye, even for just a split second. Instead, we stay in our comfort zones, scroll endlessly down the social media feeds we don't genuinely care about, stick our headphones in, and hide away from the world and any potential interaction. After all, imagine talking to someone and them rejecting your advances or conversation efforts!

Could you deal with that kind of rejection?

Well, I always thought the answer was no. I couldn't deal with it. I remember being in college, and there was a girl in the same course, but in a different class, and she was beautiful. I loved everything about her. Her voice. Her way with words. I was smitten in a way that was like nothing I had felt before. But did I speak to her once? No, of course not.

I wasn't confident enough to make the first move. And who knows, maybe she wasn't confident enough to make the first move with me but felt the same way. In a situation like this, you've got two people who want to have a deep and meaningful connection with each other. Yet neither of them has the confidence to say hi. When you think about that from a bird's-eye view, doesn't that seem ridiculous?

A friend of mine was the opposite. A few years back, he was really into the computer game *League of Legends*. You play with five other people on your team and can play with friends, or you can play with strangers on the internet. He played with someone, and they did well, winning a few games back to back.

They would talk over voice chat while playing, and it turns out the player was a girl. They eventually shared phone numbers, added each other on social media, and ended up dating for over a year. How crazy is that? The chances that they would be paired together, logging onto the computer game at exactly the right time to get paired up, out of 160 million other worldwide players, is practically impossible.

But then they managed to enjoy each other's company and have such a beautiful relationship with one another. They're not together now because of difficult mental health issues that were getting in the way, but they're still very close friends who chat every week and still play together from time to time. Isn't that beautiful?

These two human beings enjoyed each other's company because one of them made the first move, which allowed the relationship to blossom into something amazing that they both share. This brings me nicely to method numero two: always make the first move.

The Science for Taking the First Step

As human beings, we're conditioned to fear rejection. We're social animals, and it's in our million-year-old instinct to stay a part of the pack. Human beings couldn't survive on their own. If you're wandering around the wildernesses of 1000 BC and you get sick or injure yourself, then chances are you're going to die. On the other hand, if you have your tribe around you, they can look after you, and you can look after them (more on this reciprocation nature later, by the way!). You're more likely to survive.

However, as time has progressed and we no longer live in tribes of 50 people or so, but instead have the ability to connect with literally millions of people across the internet, all judging and criticizing everything all the time, we're trained ourselves to hate rejection. In fact, we do everything we can to not risk being rejected at all, and that means we stop ourselves from taking that first, potentially embarrassing, and painful step.

If I had spoken to the girl I fancied at college and said, "Hey, want to get to know each other? I think you're cute," and she went "Urgh, get away from me, loser!" then yeah, I'm probably going to feel a little crushed. But, time being the best medicine, I would eventually get over it. Sure, the experience would then tell me not to do it again because 100% of the time I had been crushed, but think about how many friends you have had in your life.

You've spoken to them all for the first time at one point, so it's safe to say rejection doesn't happen all the time. As human beings are once more conditioned, we always remember the negative things that happen far more than we do the positives, which is why you need to consciously spend effort in thinking positively. This is another great reason why you should practice smiling to yourself more; to think more positively!

So, going back to taking the first step. Everyone is afraid of taking the first step, but in almost all situations, if you can do it, then you've taken the risk off of that other person, put them at ease, and now that first barrier is out of the way, you can start building your relationship with them.

Psychologists Steven Asher and Sherri Oden carried out a study that proves this to be the case. They studied elementary school children to see how they made friends with other children and how they were accepted, thus overcoming the fear of rejection.

They discovered one of the most important and essential skills a child needs to have when trying to make new friends and form new relationships is the ability to initiate an engagement—aka, taking that first step in communicating with another human being.

In this study, sure, the kids were inviting other kids to come and play in the fort castle or wanted to see if the other girl wanted to come and play with the same doll. If you have kids or have been around children, then you know that they'll do this. They'll bring over a toy to someone and see if you want to play together, and this is the foundation for the new relationship.

Of course, I'm not saying you need to invite your work colleagues over to play in a pillow fort together (some workplaces have rules against that kind of behavior), but there are more adult ways of taking that first step.

Action Time – Take the First Step

I know what you're thinking, and I understand. It's hard to take the first step because you need a certain degree of confidence, and the pressures of being rejected can leave you feeling absolutely crushed, sometimes even paralyzed. I know. I've been there myself, and you may truly believe there's no other way to be.

I'm going to talk more about being confident and ways to boost this way of thinking in future chapters, but I want you to start small for now. By starting small, you can build up your confidence over time with little wins, and then this kind of personal development will really start to snowball. This is how it worked for me, as I'm sure it can work for you too.

When I say starting small, I mean to make the first move in small situations. This could be talking to the cashier in the shop. It only has to be small talk, but use the opportunity to practice. You can speak to the people around you in a queue, people at work, and even the people you live with. Keep building up your confidence and having these small interactions, and soon you'll be able to talk to anyone about anything, right from the time you meet them.

Over time, you'll get better and better at doing this, which will lead to the confidence you need to make deep, meaningful relationships and come across as the most confident, charismatic version of yourself possible. However, this isn't the only way to start a relationship. There's one more I want to talk about before moving on.

Method 3 – Excuse Me. Can You Help Me?

"The power of asking is the key to abundance living." –
Lailah Gifty Akita

There are a few things to think about when it comes to connecting with other people. You need trust on both sides. You need confidence. You need the ability to speak, make the first move, and create some kind of connection that will lead to friendship and beyond. While it may sound a little against the fray, one of the best ways to do this, psychologically speaking, is to ask someone for a favor.

Now, obviously, I'm not saying you'll sit next to someone on the train, start speaking to them, and then ask them to stay in your house to look after your dog. There are clearly big favors and small favors, but asking for a favor can be a great way to start and develop a relationship with someone.

Allow me to explain.

When you ask someone for a favor, you're not just asking for help from someone, but it's more the fact you're specifically asking the person you're asking. Let's say you're at work, and you're starting on a project for a new client. You have some ideas, but you're not sure which direction you want to take. What do you do?

Well, one thing you could do is ask for advice or a suggestion from a coworker. This is not only a sign of intimacy, but more importantly, it's a sign of trust. You're saying to that other person, hey, I respect you and your opinion, and I trust your judgment on this topic. Can you impart some of your wisdom to me? Obviously, you're not saying this out loud, but the fact you're asking for it implies that this is how you feel. After all, you're not going to ask someone for their opinion if you don't care for it, nor have any interest in that other person and their thoughts.

This means you've already suggested the foundations of a friendship, and if people think you like them (because you're not going to ask for a favor if you don't), then they'll already feel positively towards you. This then leads to a connection, and so on.

A Harvard study titled "Very Happy People" found there was a 0.7 correlation between people giving social support and their happiness. This means that the more people help other people, giving rather than taking, the happier they are. Just as a gauge, a 0.7 correlation is a higher correlation than the one between smoking and cancer.

This is why people get married. Because you're living your life together, you're supporting each other, through thick and thin. You help each other out with daily tasks, inspiring each other to live your best lives, and generally being there for each other when you need them.

Making People Feel Good

The benefits of asking someone for help are endless when it comes to relationships. A study in human relations by Jon Decker found that asking for a favor helps boost the other person's self-esteem, and, in turn, they will like you more.

As human beings, we're wired to want to belong to a group of other people. We are social creatures. No human being wants to be an outcast from the group, and all humans want to be accepted. This includes acceptance for what they're able to bring to the table, both in terms of actions and ideas. It's like you're tapping into this area of the mind by asking for favors because you're ticking all the boxes. People you ask favors to feel secure and as though they belong. You're accepting them.

It also makes people feel capable because you're asking them since you believe they're capable of doing whatever it is you're asking them to do. This is a huge boost to their self-esteem and self-confidence, which comes from you, increasing how much of a positive light they see you in.

All of these are essential when it comes to making friends and making people feel good about themselves.

Action Time – Asking for Small, Suitable Favors

So, now we've gone through why asking for favors can be a great method for connecting with other people, it's time to put it all into action. As I said in the introduction of this chapter, you're not going to ask a complete stranger to look after your house for you, so start with small favors suitable for the people you're talking to.

For example, if you need help moving house or looking for a lift to the airport, you could ask a coworker. Thank them, maybe get them something to thank them from your vacation, and the favor is sorted. However, while this is, in essence, a quick favor, this interaction can do so much for building up your relationship with that person. Another example we've already spoken about is asking people for their ideas.

Whether you're working on a project at work, looking for vacation ideas, in need of a package to be picked up, or need a lift somewhere, these are all ideas you can use that are deemed acceptable for asking someone you may not know too well.

As your relationships start to get more trustworthy and meaningful, you can ask for more favors, such as babysitting your child, looking after a pet for the weekend, and things like this. Don't confuse this with having to always ask for favors if you don't need them. If you're just asking for favors just because you can, this isn't genuine, and it's not the best way to build a new relationship.

If you need help with something or are looking to open the doors to someone new in your life, making them feel welcomed, accepted, and appreciated, this is the best method to use every time. And with that, we come to the end of part one! What do you think so far? Have you learned some great ways to start speaking to people? This is, of course, the first step to being the charismatic and confident version of yourself, so make sure you get creative with how you use these methods and keep practicing them!

Moreover, and more excitingly, we're now moving into part two, where we're going to focus on a few of the methods you can use to deepen this connection to someone once you've started to get to know them. It's all about how you can take a relationship of any level, and turn it into a deep and meaningful one.

Part Two – Sowing the Seeds for Something Beautiful

I love the phrasing of this chapter: *Sowing the seeds for something beautiful.* I know I wrote it, but when you think about it in the way that it relates to a relationship, it creates these beautiful images in your head of what a relationship in your own life can look like. It can be a friendship, a romantic relationship, a relationship with your parents, or even a professional relationship.

All relationships can be beautiful in their own way.

However, you need to get there first. When I first started dating, as I was working on tackling my social anxiety, I spent a lot of time tackling the things we spoke about in Part One. I was building up my confidence and making the first move when I met people. This was particularly evident in my dating life. I was working on being able to talk to girls and could ask them on a date, and that was fine. It took practice, but I got there.

Then it came to the date itself, and this was an entirely new ball game.

There's so much of a difference between talking to someone for the first time and talking to them again, getting to know them, and moving forward with this. I've dedicated the next five chapters to this part. We're going to explore five powerful methods that can help

29

you build relationships, improve your charisma, win friends, and deepen your connections with other people.

Method 4 – Mastering the Art of Listening

"When people talk, listen completely. Most people never listen." – Ernest Hemingway

You've probably heard about this point before, but being able to listen to someone is one of the most important skills you can have when it comes to building a connection with someone. I'm sure you have been in a situation where you've been talking to someone about something you're interested in and excited about, but it doesn't feel like that other person is listening.

Maybe they're playing on their phone, looking out a window, or just everything about them, and their body language, says they don't care. I'm sure you remember times like this now, or someone you know who does this. Take a moment to think about how this feels.

How do you feel? Do you feel sad? Pushed away? Ignored? Unaccepted? As though what you have to say is not good enough or worth their time? However you feel, the feelings aren't good, and not listening to people and making them feel this way is not going to win you any friends whatsoever.

That being said, the opposite is true.

If you give someone your full attention and make them feel as though they're being listened to and that you genuinely care about what they're saying, you're going to make them feel happy, accepted, belonging, and as though you have a connection with them. This is why listening is so important when it comes to making friends.

Carl Rogers, a renowned American psychologist, famously stated that active and deep listening is at the very core of a healthy relationship. Through the art of listening, you'll be able to encourage strength and growth in any relationship, and people who are heard are less likely to be defensive and will be more open to new ideas themselves.

This means that not only will people be happier and more connected to you if you listen to them, but it will also increase the chances that they'll be listening to you. This is how a happy, two-way relationship is formed.

The Two Types of Listening

A study carried out in 2003 by Faye Doell discovered two main types of listening a person can do, three if you count not actually listening, but pretending to. If you're actively listening to someone speak, you're doing one of two things. You're either A, listening to understand the other person, or B, listening to respond to the other person.

How many times have you been in a conversation, and you already know what you're going to say before the other person has even finished talking? Yeah, I'm sure we all have at some point. This usually happens in arguments or heated discussions where you may not agree with what someone is saying, and they say their point, and you'll respond with something like "Yeah, but...", and then you'll go straight into your point.

This is listening to respond because you're not really listening; you're more waiting for the other person to finish, so you can have your say. This will not make the other person feel heard, and this is where your relationship will fall apart.

On the other hand, if you listen to understand, you're really taking the opportunity to listen to what the other person is saying and how they feel. Based on what they say, you then form a response that pushes the conversation further, whether you're asking a question for a greater understanding of what they're saying, or you're accepting what they're saying and then bringing up a counterpoint.

The same studies show that people who tend to listen to understand experience much greater and more satisfying relationships. Suppose you're the sort of person who wants to "fix" other people, while your intentions are good. In that case, you are perhaps most of the time listening to respond because you're flexing your desire to influence others, and this leads to you not actually listening to the other, but again listening to respond.

To cut a long story short, if you want better, more satisfying relationships where you're listened to properly, and you're happier with the people you're connected with, you need to learn how to listen to understand.

Action Time – How to Become a Better Listener

While many of us, you included, may have some bad habits when it comes to listening to others, everyone can become a better listener by practicing a few key points. The more you practice these points, the better you'll become, and therefore the better the relationships you'll have. Let's get into them.

Empathizing with the Speaker

First, and always a great way to become a better listener instantly, is to put yourself inside the mind of the person you're listening to. Become the person who is talking. This can bring so much more compassion and empathy into your conversations because you can resonate and understand what is being said.

For example, let's say someone comes to talk to you, and they've had a bad day at work. They made a mistake on a project, and they're worried about getting fired. You could listen to respond and have all these ideas on how things will get better, or they could redeem their mistake or advice on how to accept the situation they're in.

On the other hand, you can listen to understand and feel that yes, they are worried, and while they believe they may be getting fired, you can ask further questions to see whether that's likely, or what they think they can do to make things better. This is listening to understand, and it's far more helpful to approach a situation in this way.

Coupled with this point, you'll want to think about the meaning behind what the person is saying. This can be obvious, and other times it may be subtle, but listening for the meaning behind why someone is saying something will help you understand them tenfold.

When you take note of the tone of voice someone is saying something and the inflection they have on their words, you'll be able to further identify what they're saying to you. If I say, "Yeah, I hope you have a good day," this could mean anything, whether I'm nice or super passive-aggressive, depending on my tone of voice.

Be Accepting and Non-Judgmental

Alan Watts famously speaks about how no human being knows anything in many of his talks, and it's true. At the end of the day, none of us know what's going on in the universe, and when it comes to the happenings of somebody's life, there's never a right or wrong answer. We are not the authorities of what is happening.

That being said, it's so important to make sure you're not judgmental when people are talking to you, or you at least try to be as non-judgmental as you can be, and I know that's easier said than done. However, if you can master this, you'll become an amazing listener because you're concentrating on what the person is saying rather than focusing on your preconceived judgments.

This can be difficult. When someone is talking about something you're passionate about or have strong feelings towards, then you may already have ideas that the other person is stupid or has no idea what they're talking about, which means you'll find yourself wrapped up in these thoughts, rather than listening to the person who's speaking. In essence, you're listening to respond, rather than listening to understand.

Of course, you're allowed to have opinions on things, and you're allowed to disagree with people, but in many cases, there's a lot of context that you may not know or understand as to why someone is saying what they're saying. If you can pay attention to this, rather than forming your own opinions in your head and making judgments, then your listening skills, and therefore your relationships with people, will skyrocket.

A Note on Body Language

There's no denying that body language is important when it comes to listening, and any kind of guide to communication you read or listen to will talk about body language. When listening, a great way to improve how much attention you're paying to the other person is to make eye contact with them. We seem to be living in a time where this is much harder than it first seems, and when I was in the depths of suffering from social anxiety, I literally couldn't do it.

However, it was a skill I was able to implement into my life with practice, and it made my relationships so much stronger. Regarding your body language, nodding is a great way to keep someone engaged with you while they're talking to you, and it non-verbally confirms that you want them to carry on and that you're interested in what they have to say.

You'll also want to pay attention to the speaker's body language. What are they doing, and where are they looking? Are they making eye contact with you, or are they looking everywhere else? Do they look fidgety and unsure of what they're saying, or are they confident and holding their own? Body language says so much about us all, and reading it will bring such a deeper dimension to your interactions.

And with that, our trip into the world of listening concludes. Like every other aspect and method of this book, this is all the information you need to know. It's just a case of sticking with it and putting it into practice. Start small and work on some of these tips over time, and you'll start to see some big changes in your life.

In case you were wondering, no, a relationship doesn't just mean you need to sit and listen to what someone has to say in silence. You get lots of chances to speak too, which is what we're going to explore now!

Method 5 – Improving the Flow of Conversion

"Nothing trumps good conversation." – Rich Eisen

In the previous chapters, we've spoken a lot about introducing yourself to someone and how to start a conversation. The last chapter was about how you can listen to what another person says to give them your full attention. But there's one crucial piece of the puzzle missing.

What do you actually talk about?

It's all well and good having the courage to speak up and shake hands with another person, but if you can't take a conversation from there, and you end up stalling, sitting in awkward silences, and just being very distant in general, both you and the person you're speaking to are not going to have a nice or memorable conversation, at least not in a positive way. The chances are if they remember you for being awkward, or perhaps even boring, then you're not going to come across as charismatic, and they're not going to want to be your friend. Yeah, those are some hard truths.

First up, however, this isn't something you should worry about. While going through my self-improvement journey, at least at the beginning, there were at least a dozen times where I would fall into this situation. I remember when I was trying to speak to girls (I know, that classic chestnut, don't judge me!), and I was so confident and charismatic at the beginning.

We really hit it off and laughed and chatted about something that was happening across the road, but then something shifted, and neither of us knew what to say or how to carry the conversation on. It basically ended up with us having some awkward goodbyes and never seeing each other again. There's no denying I felt a little dumb initially, but hey, I'm still here, and that was years ago. If it happens to you, you may feel a little embarrassed for the rest of the day, but you'll get over it, and life will always go on.

Always try and remember this when you can. Practice makes perfect, so the more you put yourself in these situations, firstly the hardier you'll become to them going wrong, but secondly, and most importantly, the better you'll be at holding your own in a conversation with anyone. This is what I'm going to be focusing on in this chapter.

We're going to be talking about the art of conversational flow, which means the grace and lucidity in which you can traverse different topics, how effortlessly and confidently you can keep talking, and how to have conversations where when you both walk away, you're left with a smile on your face thinking, *Wow, that was a really good conversation!*

We've already spoken about the importance of listening, but don't forget that that is a massive part of having a conversation. These are some of the other points you'll need to be thinking about.

Be Open and Honest

First things first: ALWAYS be open and honest in your conversations. Within us all, there is sometimes a bit of ego that wants to be validated, and we may feel the need to emphasize certain facts about our lives or make something sound much better than it actually was to make ourselves seem better or lucky or whatever to the person we're speaking to.

This never works. When someone is talking to you and starts boasting or exaggerating things, I think you'll agree that it's really easy to spot. You might not think about it at the time, but you'll get the feeling that something is not right or the person is putting on airs. Validating your ego to someone else is not the best way to connect and try to make friends with someone. In fact, some people would probably agree it's the worst, so avoid it at all costs.

The science behind this has been written about in a book titled *The (Honest) Truth About Dishonesty* by Dan Ariely. Here, he writes about how human beings can believe themselves to be honest, all while telling little lies or dishonest truths. Think about yourself right now and who you are. The chances are you think of yourself as an honest person, even though you almost definitely lie about little things in your life.

However, since you will mainly tell lies over little things you believe don't matter, you'll see yourself as an honest person. Don't worry, I'm not calling you a dishonest person since this is the way that most people go through life. If you're not feeling okay, but you don't want to talk about it, you may say everything's fine when it's not. You may say you don't know something when you do, or you may lie about something you do know when in reality, you're not sure.

So why do we do it?

Well, no matter which way you look at it, we're all telling lies, no matter how small they are, for one main reason: to protect ourselves.

You protect yourself from embarrassment, to protect your interests and to get what you want, to protect your self-image and the way others see you, to protect your assets and the things you have, including your energy levels and the time you don't want to waste on doing something else, or to protect the emotions and feelings of others.

Lying is just a way to manipulate reality so you can protect the way you see "good and right" in the world. You have an image of what you believe to be the right way of doing things, so you lie to maintain that reality. Interesting when you see it like that, isn't it?

Let's say you're at the gym, and people are talking about the polarizing topic of politics. However, while you're a firm supporter of the blue side, it seems everyone in the room supports red. What do you do? Do you lie and say you support the red side because you want to fit in and out of fear of being judged? Or do you say you support the blue side because it's truly who you are?

What about lying and not saying your truth to protect others' feelings, perhaps if you're afraid of hurting their feelings or making them not like you because they won't agree with what you have to say?

In the book *Nutureshock*, by Po Bronson and Ashley Merryman, they write about how parents will lie to their children about the most trivial things and that children will lie to their parents far more often than their parents will realize. This is because children believe they are telling their parents what they want to hear, and this will make them happier, like whether you've stolen some extra chocolate biscuits out of the cupboard or not.

This continues throughout many stages of your life, all stemming from when we were children. Children believe that their parents have these massive, unfulfillable expectations of them and that if they're not fulfilling them, it's going to make them sad, so they lie about what's going on. The research also found that if parents forcefully confront the lying to their younger children, this only convinces them to try to get better at lying.

If you want to make friends, you need to work on being yourself, which means stopping all the little lies and just being honest. This means standing up for what you believe in and being true to yourself and your beliefs. If you're able to do this, then eventually, you'll connect with people who share the same beliefs as you, and this is where true relationships are formed.

Speak for Longer Than Normal

When you're talking, how long are the answers you give? When I was starting out with talking to people, I remember when someone would ask me a question, I always believed that people didn't really care about what I had to say and were more interested in themselves. I felt as though that most of the time, people were just asking because it was the polite thing to do, but then if you think that people are thinking this way, are you going to want friendships with them? Probably not.

When you're answering questions that people have for you, and this point leans into the just be yourself point above, answer the question with detail, giving the other person time to relate and keep the flow of conversation going. For example, saying your favorite movie is *The Matrix* and that's it doesn't open the floor to more conversation. In many cases, people will probably think you're just being blunt.

"Hey man, what's your favorite sport?" says the guy at the gym you're making small talk with in the changing room. "Treadmill," you reply. Great conversation. Everyone loves to be a part of it. Instead, how about trying something like this:

"Hey man, what's your favorite sport?"

"It's running on the treadmill at the moment, which is actually quite surprising because I used to hate running. I loved it as a kid but haven't done it for ages and for some reason just really find it enjoyable. Is that weird?"

See how much more personality this approach has, rather than just giving blunt, unfollowable answers? You're showcasing so much more of yourself, are being so much more confident, and bringing so much to the table. The person you're speaking to also has so much more conversational points to work with. Are they going to agree? Say they've also loved and hated it? Do they hate it? Do they understand your newfound love for it? And so on.

The Art of Charm website states that when talking to someone, always aim for two-sentence answers, as a rule of thumb, and one of the best tips to remember is to answer the question directly and then add the "why" to your answer. It's an easy way to have a proper conversation and give the other person something to respond to.

This is such a great tip to remember because not only will you be having a charismatic, confident

45

conversation, but you'll also be learning lots about yourself and why you think the way you do, which will give you even more confidence in yourself!

Asking the Right Questions

The final point to think about when it comes to keeping the flow of conversation, well, flowing, is to make sure that you're not just talking about yourself the whole time, but you're asking questions to dive deeper into the other person's life, and showing a genuine interest in what they have to say and the person that they are as an individual.

I remember when I started going to the gym, and there was a guy in there who was always in the swimming pool at the same time as me. He used to swim professionally when he was younger, many years ago, and all he would do was always talk about himself. Now, I didn't mind so much at the time because I didn't like talking about myself, but he was so boring. He would go on and on about swimming and the best way to breaststroke and how to train and what to eat and what he did for his job and his wife and kids and how politics is crazy and so on. It was so boring because not once did he ever ask a question about me or my life. Come to think of it, I don't think he knew a single thing about me over the few months we spoke.

I'm sure you don't need me to point out that there are people like this everywhere in life, and the chances are very high that you know someone who fits this description. What do you think about that person? Sure, they're not bad people, but there's no connection or friendship there. It's just you and whoever is sitting around listening to this other person talk. If you don't want to be that person, then you've got to start asking questions.

I wrote the heading for this section as asking the right questions, and hopefully, that got you thinking about what sort of questions you could be asking. The truth is, there are no right or wrong questions, but when it comes to making friends and helping people to connect with you, there's a type of question that knocks every other question out of the ballpark, and that's opinion questions.

How good does it make you feel when someone asked for your opinion on something that matters to them? It feels very good. Just like when you're asking someone for a favor, and this shows that you trust that other person, asking for someone's opinion works along the same lines. You're saying, "I value your opinion and your thoughts, and I want to hear them." It's this view that the other person has that you're interested in what they have to say that's going to bring you together.

Try it yourself. If you're trying to think of a movie to watch, a restaurant to go to, a way to approach a project, or which TV series or book you want to binge next, get someone else's opinion and see the conversation start to flow.

As with all the points we've spoken about throughout this chapter, the best way to keep a conversation flowing is to focus on the other person and put them at the center of the conversation. Whether you're asking them questions about themselves, asking for their opinion, or just hearing what they have to say, this is a method where you can't go wrong.

However, this isn't a method that's going to work with everyone. In fact, none of the methods you could ever learn about and try will work with everyone because you simply can't be friends with everyone. You need to find people who have similar interests to you and are, in essence, a reflection of yourself.

Method 6 – Discovering the Reflection of Yourself

"Friendship is born at that moment when one person says to another, 'What! You too? I thought I was the only one.'"
– *C.S. Lewis*

This is absolutely, 100%, certainly, beyond a doubt, one of the most important aspects of having a relationship with any human being on the planet. Whether that's with a friend, partner, parent, coworker, and so on, this is where you must have some kind of common ground.

There are nearly ten billion people on the planet, and that's a ton of diversity out there, and not everyone will be on the same page as you.

Think back to tribal times when humans were all living off the land, hunting, and gathering, and trying to survive day in and day out. At these times, we all share the common interest of surviving, whether that's hunting for food or looking after the children, so it's easy to work together and towards a common goal. This progresses further as civilization develops.

Some people want to sail boats, and some people want to conquer other lands. Some people want to be farmers and raise families, and some want to be explorers or artists. In the modern day, some people like certain genres of music and movies and not others.

Some people love money and fast cars, and others like to walk down more spiritual paths and practice minimalism and so on.

What I'm saying is that it's hardwired into us to seek out people who have similar interests and beliefs as us. Thus, with every new interaction you have, your brain is trying to find a reflection of itself in the other people that you're speaking to. One study published in the *Social Cognitive and Affective Neuroscience Journal* confirmed that common ground is the first thing we look for on a psychological and neurological level when looking to make a connection.

In their studies, they took a group of people and gave them small electrical shocks. Some of the people were friends, and some people were strangers, and the whole time their brain activity was being monitored. As it turns out, when someone else is being shocked, the brain responds in different ways depending on who that person is.

If the person being shocked is a stranger, the brain barely reacts. However, if the person being shocked is a friend, the brain responds in basically an identical way to if *you* were being shocked. Coan, one of the leaders of the project, said:

"The correlation between self and friend was remarkably similar. The findings show the brain's remarkable capacity to model self to others; that people close to us become a part of ourselves, and that

isn't just a metaphor or poetry. It's a very real, physical change that occurs."

What this means is that you are, or at least will be, part of the people you surround yourself with. Gary Vaynerchuck famously quotes that "you are the average of the five people you surround yourself with," and so having common ground with all these people is how you develop a friend group. Of course, even among your friend group, you're not going to have the exact same interests as everyone, but having some will be a foundation you need to have.

When it comes to making friends and connecting with new people, it's all about finding this common ground from which to build a relationship. Going back to my example of the guy who wouldn't shut up talking about himself when swimming, he clearly had a passionate interest in swimming, or himself. I'm not sure, but my interest was that I just enjoyed being in the water after working out. This is a slight common ground, but not enough to build a connection.

On the other hand, if we both loved the idea of competitive swimming, I'm sure we would have got on well. Think about the friends you've had throughout your life. In every relationship you've had, you've shared something in common, whether you love partying, reading, the same kind of music, and so on. It's all about finding that common ground.

Action Time – How to Find Common Ground

So, how do you find these shared interests without interviewing the people you're talking to and making your interaction feel like an interrogation? Nobody likes to be interrogated. Well, you can take a few approaches, and which one you choose will all depend on the situation you're in. Allow me to explain.

We already spoke about this first method in the last chapter, but asking questions is the best way to find common ground. However, if you're asking forward, abrupt questions, this may seem a little unnatural, so try to tone it down and make things feel as natural as possible.

For example, asking someone what their dream holiday would be is a great way to gauge what kind of person they are. Do they want to book a hotel in the mountains and go hiking, or would they rather go to a beach party in Ibiza? Sure, you're playing off stereotypes here, but the chances are if they fit the stereotype, then you can see what kind of person they are and whether you have common ground.

What people say is a reflection about themselves, so you need to make sure you're as present as possible when listening to what people have to say, their body language, and the way they talk. If you're talking about a certain subject or something like politics comes up, and the person quickly dismisses it and changes the subject, then this is an obvious sign that they either don't care about politics or don't want to talk about it.

On the other hand, say you start talking about fishing; you may see the other person's eyes light up, and they'll start talking about all these different aspects of fishing with real excitement. If this happens, then you know you've found something the other person is interested in.

We've already talked a bit about making your conversations about the other person, and the same applies here. You don't want to jump straight in and say you caught the biggest fish ever and everyone loved you, and it was amazing because you're just making the conversation about yourself. You need to edge information out of the other person.

That doesn't mean you can't talk about yourself, but instead lead with the other person. So, combining all this together, here's the kind of method you'll want to take. First, listen to what the other person is saying to get hints about what kind of interests they have. Keep chatting until there's a topic that interests you both, and then dive into, asking them questions to explain more. Add in your own stories and experiences, but not in a boasting light, but in a way that progresses the conversation.

This method is the best way to find common ground, and once established, you should see a new friendship or relationship starting to bloom right before your eyes.

Now, it should go without saying that while this is an effective technique for building and nurturing relationships, you've probably heard the saying that you can't please everyone, nor can you be friends with absolutely everyone you meet. If you tried to, then at some point, you're going to end up faking and lying about who you are in order to fit in, and that's not what we're trying to achieve here.

As you go about your life and build your confidence and begin to interact with more and more people, you're going to find people you don't like, and there are going to be people who don't like you. There's nothing wrong with this at all because you literally cannot be everyone's cup of tea, which is a British saying that means the same thing.

This means that you'll need to know how to choose your friends, and how to choose who you're spending your energy on, and who you'll engage with for a little while before deciding if you actually want some kind of relationship with them, which is what we're going to be focusing on in the next chapter!

Method 7 – Choosing the Right Friends

"Young people, choose your friends wisely. There's an old saying, show me your friends and I'll tell you who you are."
– Unknown

Choosing the right friends is never easy. While I was in school, I ended up hanging around with some kids that used to smoke drugs on the weekend, stolen from one of the boys' older brothers. I only tried it once myself, but I don't understand why I chose to hang around with them. We had nothing in common, and we didn't like each other that much, and the only time I did try it, we ended up getting a warning from the police, meaning I got in a lot of trouble when I got home.

Not every person out there will be, nor needs to, be your friend. As an individual interested in making strong relationships with people, you need to be selective with who you're creating these relationships with. You want to befriend people who are good for you and will raise you up to be the best version of yourself, especially since this is what you'll hopefully want to be doing for them.

Think about some of the people in your life now or who have been in your life in the past. We've all had toxic friends at some point; you know, the people who gossip behind everyone's back and say mean things, or perhaps even bully other friends because they think it's funny, even when no one else is laughing. Sure, everyone goes through stages, and some people will pretend to be someone they're not because they want to fit in, but as you grow up, you should start to see people for who they are.

It's strange when you think about it. In my sales company back in 2015, I worked with a guy who used to talk dirt behind everyone's back. We'd have a meeting, and someone would be nervous about giving their presentation, and afterward, he would moan and berate the person for being nervous and not being confident like he thought "all men should be." He did this with everyone about everything, and it never occurred to me that he would do the same about me.

Because he used to "open up" with all these little statements about everyone else to me, I thought we were friends, but of course, I overhear him talking about me and how annoying I am with the people he was just berating minutes beforehand, and I suddenly realized the kind of person he was. Aka, not the type of person I wanted to waste my time and energy on.

The Science Behind Choosing Friends

There's a saying I love, and while there are many different ways of wording it, it basically comes down to this one statement. Read it and read it again:

You are the people you surround yourself with.

Let's say you have a group of people around you, and there are six of you in total. Since you'll have a relationship based on things like proximity (meaning you see each other a lot, whether you're in school, at a club, or work) and common interests, you're people who know each other quite well.

However, that doesn't mean these are nice people, just because you have common interests. Look at the way these people think and how they look at the world, and you'll find that you "borrow" a bit of all of them. Some people might even say you're the average of those five people. If you haven't chosen your friendships but rather just associate with these people because they're physically close to you, they may not be the best people for you, nor may they be offering you the best kind of relationship you deserve.

This is such an important consideration you need to be thinking about because the people in this group of friends, whether obvious or not, will dictate so many aspects of your life.

A 2013 study published in *Psychological Science* found that if you're the sort of person who suffers from lack of discipline or low self-esteem, your best chances of improving these areas of your life are hanging out and interacting with people who are strong-willed and disciplined.

Likewise, the friends you keep will influence your choices massively, even if you think you're individually in control. A 2014 survey published in the *Journal of*

Consumer Research discovered that friends are a key factor in making financially sound decisions and not making impulse purchases. However, this also works the other way around.

If you love to give in to temptations and you can easily spend money, your friends can amplify this since you're more likely to indulge together. Whether you look at this from a financial, health, or social standpoint, just being around certain people can leave you in a bad position you don't want to be in. This is what it means to be partners in crime.

To cut a long story short, if you hang out and become friends with people who make bad choices and put people down, then the chances are you're going to make bad choices and put people down. If you want to lift yourself up with others and make good choices, then you'll want to hang out with people who do all these things. Science says so.

When you're looking for friends, or want any kind of relationship, whether that's professional or romantic, you need to make sure you're choosing the right person; this may seem easier said than done unless you know what you're looking for. Below, we're going to explore some ways to do just this!

Taking Things to the Next Level

Ask yourself this: Where do you want to be in five years' time? Do you want a promotion? Do you want to be fitter and healthier? Do you want to be traveling, owning your own house, or starting your own business? Whatever it is you want to achieve, the people you surround yourself with will be the people who will get you there and will help you make the right decisions.

When you're going into a new relationship, ask yourself: Is this person going to help me be the best version of myself, or will they hold me back? When I started writing these books, I had a friend who was self-employed at the same time as a personal trainer. We would hang out every Friday, having a few drinks with each other, and then just chat about all these plans and ideas for new projects we had. We were both working on different things, but having the opportunity to be open and to get excited about what we were doing only propelled us going forward, and here we are today.

Before, when I was hanging out with the stoner people for a year or two, nobody wanted to do anything and was very content staying in the same place they had always been in and had no aspirations to do anything. That's fine if that's what they wanted to do, but it wasn't for me. It was making me miserable.

Be selective with who you want to be and get people who can help you get there. Naturally, you'll also be having the same effect on their life. That's not to say you can't talk to anyone outside of your friendships. It's all well and good to have acquaintance friends and people you just have small talk with and just relax, maybe have a drink with every once in a while. There's nothing wrong with that. You need to be thinking about who your close friends are and who you're going to give the time and energy to while allowing them into your inner circle.

Finding Yourself in Others

Hand in hand with the last point and the last chapter (so don't worry, I'm not going to go on about it too much more!), finding out what your friend's goals and aspirations are is a great way to see if you could and should be friends. This is why it's so important to find common ground. If you're both able to aim towards the same aspiring goals, then you're going to be able to lift each other up, and you'll have a lot more in common, even if your goals are two different things.

Choose friends with big goals that are on a similar or higher level to your own. These don't even have to be things like starting a business, writing a book, or traveling the world. If you're just coming out of depression, for example, you may just have the goal of getting a social life with people you see regularly, or you may want to form the habits of exercising and looking after your health properly. Choosing friends with similar values will help you achieve your goals, no matter what they are.

Choose Friends That Give and Take

A friendship, or any relationship for that matter, is all about give and take. It's a balancing act. You can't have a relationship where one person does everything for the other person, whether that's in the form of money, time, or emotional support, but gets nothing back. That's not to say you should be giving with the idea that you're going to get something back at some point, but your relationship won't be balanced, and you'll be left feeling unfulfilled. Eventually, you'll be filled with resentment for yourself and them.

This means you need to give what you expect to get and treat others how you would want to be treated yourself. This is the golden rule of friendships. If you can manage this and reduce the number of people who aren't treating you like you deserve, you'll find the relationships you have to be far more rewarding.

Action Time – Get the Relationships You Deserve

The action times I've shared so far have all been about finding new friends and building the confidence to talk to people, but this one will be a bit different. This time I want you to take a look at the relationships you already have and start thinking about whether they are the relationships you want or deserve. Don't worry, I'm not saying you should say, "Oh, my girlfriend is pretty toxic, so I'm out." You don't need to be so reckless with your decisions, but take a moment to evaluate how you feel with the people you're spending time with.

You may find you're still friends with people you went to school or college with, but you've grown apart and don't have a lot in common anymore. You just hang out because it's your comfort zone to be together. Like I said earlier in the chapter, it's fine to have these friends. You're not trying to cut people out and say you're done with them, but you're considering how much of your time you're giving them.

If you're giving them all your time and you're hanging out multiple times per week, but you're not happy and want to instead spend your time with people who are more like you, then you'll need to cut back and find these new relationships that are more suited to who you are in your life right now.

However, if you find that you're friends with someone who's pretty toxic, you may want to start moving away from them completely. Don't worry; you're not alone in this. There are plenty of people out there, me included, who end up being friends with people who are pretty toxic, but you don't even see it until you think about it and open your eyes.

The truth is, most "toxic" people aren't toxic for the sake of being toxic, but rather they are hurt and dealing with a lot of emotional pain or baggage, perhaps stuff they have to deal with from past relationships or even from their relationships with their parents. However, these traumas are up to them to sort out, and it's no excuse for being a bad person.

This is where the decision-making process comes into play. Are you going to be friends with these people and support them on their journey, even if it gets worse before it gets better, or are you going to cut back the amount of time you're spending with them to focus on other relationships? The choice is up to you.

These can feel like big decisions to make. If you take some time to think about your partner and think, "Actually, this person isn't right for me," this can be a hard state of mind to come to terms with. In this situation, give it time and let things play out on their own accord. Everything will happen the way it's meant to. Just give it some thinking time, talk to the other person about how you feel in the relationship, and allow yourself to see what is really going on.

This way, you'll be opening the door to beautiful, balanced, and fulfilling relationships, where you're investing your time on the right people that are best suited for you while still allowing yourself to be civil with everybody else!

And with that, we come to the end of this chapter. As promised, this part of the book is all about sowing the seeds to beautiful relationships, whether that's becoming more confident in yourself or creating opportunities for these relationships to manifest in the first place. However, I've spoken a lot about talking and ways you can approach conversations.

There's one key part of any relationship that we haven't spoken about yet, and you may want to strap yourself in for this one because it's perhaps the most important one yet.

Method 8 – Share Experiences. Make Memories.

"We do not remember days, we remember moments." –
Cesare Pavese

Think of all the best relationships in your life. Scratch that, think of one relationship you've had in your life that meant something to you and was the most beautiful relationship you can think of. It can be about anyone at any time in your life. Have you got one? Nice.

Now think about what kind of relationship you had with that person. Did you go for coffee once a week, but this was the only time you saw them? Did you only ever see that person at work? Did you just see them now and then and have a phone catch up? No, the answer is probably not for all of the above. In reality, the chances are that when you think of the most beautiful relationship possible, you're thinking of relationships where you shared experiences and made memories together.

Remember the concerts you went to, the parties, the sleepovers, the all-night gaming sessions, the dates, the trips to the zoo, and the restaurants, and the vacations abroad, and crying with fits of laughter with each other, and so on? It's all well and good talking the talk and knowing *how* to talk to people, but so much of a connection will come from the experiences you share with each other.

As someone who wants to win friends and become more charismatic, it's up to you to create opportunities for these kinds of experiences to happen, which means training yourself to become a little more outgoing, confident in asking, and becoming a little more creative with the ideas you can come up with to do things. Ready for this one? Let's do it.

The Science of Making Memories and, Therefore, Great Relationships

What I love most about this concept is just how easy it is to grasp. The human brain may be infinitely complex, and we may not even understand half of how it works, but how it works on the surface is extremely simple. According to *Psychology Today,* friendships exist when pleasure is taken in the company of other people.

Whenever you do something in your life, your brain actively responds to it by releasing chemicals that make you feel good or bad about whatever situation you're in. If your body is hungry, it gives you hungry feelings. You then eat, and your body gives you feel-good chemicals like dopamine that reward you for taking action. Your brain wants you to survive, so it makes you feel good for carrying out essential tasks. With me so far?

These processes far exceed just basic survival tasks. Humans are social creatures who rely on the closeness and community of others around them. Just like feeling hungry, your mind rewards you for spending time with people because being social is hardwired into the survival part of our brain.

Now, we've come a long way from living in caves and needing each other to survive. It is very possible nowadays to live by yourself and thrive completely alone, but your brain will still make you feel lonely and release chemicals and hormones like cortisol, the stress chemical, because it wants you to interact with other people and be social. That's just human instinct.

Zeroing in on this subject a little more, if you have bad experiences with someone, like a bully or someone who beats you up or calls you names, your brain will record these experiences as being bad and will want to do everything it can to keep you away from them. This is why when you painfully break up with an ex, seeing them can bring up all those old, sad feelings that can make you feel quite strange, especially if you're not over them.

You may have agreed that you wanted to stay friends, but your brain still feels abandoned or betrayed by your ex, and will send signals to the rest of you that make you sad and, therefore, want to stay away from them. Of course, like everything we've spoken about in this book so far, and what we're going to focus on for the rest of this chapter, is that it works the other way too.

If you have a positive, fulfilling, and rewarding experience with someone, then your brain will release a ton of feel-good chemicals that record the experience as being good and the people involved as being people you want to spend more time with. It's funny because when you look at human beings in this way, it's easy to see we haven't gone very far from the kinds of people we used to be living in tribes and living off the land.

This is why typical activities you do with friends include going out to eat food or getting a takeaway delivered and then having a movie night. You could do something a bit more exhilarating, like going to a music concert, going on an assault course, or going on vacation to a beautiful place. Your mind loves all these new experiences and thrives off doing new things, expanding your comfort zone, and having a stress-free and pleasurable time, and it remembers the people you're doing these things with.

So, bringing all of this together, solid and fulfilling relationships require positive experiences. These could be anything from going somewhere or doing an activity together, or even being there for someone during a hard time. Being the person who turns negative experiences into positive experiences is another great way to build relationships, but you can't rely on this to happen. Focus on creating positive experiences from scratch.

From a science and psychology standpoint, positive experiences will relate to you as being a positive influence in the lives of the people you surround yourself with, and relationships can then grow over time.

Action Time – Go Out and Have Fun

Perhaps my favorite action time of this book.

For this method, I want you to take someone you're friends with (it doesn't matter whether you're close or you're coworkers), and you want to get closer to them and take the plunge doing something together. If you're just starting out, then start off small. This could be asking someone to go for lunch or a coffee one afternoon. If you're more confident or closer to someone, you could go for a day out together, perhaps to the beach or the zoo. You could even go for a walk in a local park.

The essence of this part of the process is that it doesn't matter what you're doing. It's more the fact you're doing something with the other person. Of course, it's good to lose yourself in the activity you're doing, but take some time to be mindful, especially afterward, about how you felt towards that person during the activity and how your bond with them is now stronger.

When people say the proof is in the pudding, this is all you're going to need, and having a few experiences like this will be a huge boost in your confidence and will show you the power of positive experiences. As a quick note, hand in hand with the previous chapters, try to take some time to pick a good activity that will suit both of you and will be something you both enjoy (common interests), or allow them to choose something to do and know they're going to like (putting them first).

Enjoy yourself and have fun, but I can't stress enough how important it is to look back at the end of the day and see how you feel about the day and the person you spent it with. This is how you'll learn and truly understand what a difference it can make.

And with that, we come to the end of Part Two. Are you enjoying yourself so far? Are you learning lots? With everything we've discussed so far, you should have everything you need to meet new people, nurturing relationships with the people around you, and to start building up your confidence by knowing what to do around new people.

While we've covered the basics, as we head into Part Three, we're going to start looking more into the advanced strategies that go into taking existing relationships and then making them stronger than ever before.

Part Three – The Advanced Teachings of Nurturing Stronger Relationships

Before I dive into the meat of this chapter, I want you to think about this question: What does a strong relationship mean to you?

To many, it means trusting each other, having respect for each other, having fun with each other, and being there for one another when you need each other. You want to feel safe and secure with this other person, and you'll want to understand each other. Perhaps it means inspiring each other or being committed to each other. Maybe it means sticking by each other no matter what.

No matter what a strong relationship means to you, the truth is that the foundations of a relationship don't come from the relationship and connection you have with someone else, but they instead come from within you. Take a moment to process that.

Suppose you're not comfortable, confident, and truly yourself with yourself. In that case, you can't expect you to be you when you're around other people, and a truly, meaningful relationship is never then going to form. Think of it this way. When you're out and about in your life, let's say you're at work, a parcel might get delivered. The person comes in, and you start chatting with them. You talk about the weather and stuff happening around you, and you put on a friendly voice, and it's a pleasant interaction.

This is what is known as "putting on airs" because it doesn't matter how you're feeling. Whether you're feeling super positive, super negative, or somewhere in between, you're going to act the same. While this is pretty understandable to act this way for someone you're probably never going to see again or will only see in passing, some of us do this to the people closest to us.

Hands up if you feel like you sometimes wear a metaphorical mask when you're hanging out with the people around you, and you don't feel like you're acting like your true self. Perhaps you act posher or politer than you are, or you talk in a certain way about particular subjects you wouldn't usually talk about because you think that's what the other person cares about, even if you don't. Maybe you filter yourself and the way you usually act because it may seem inappropriate.

Sure, there are times when this is acceptable, and you're going to need to do it, but if you want proper relationships with people, then you need to be yourself and not have to hide behind masks or filters. This can be hard, I know from experience, but it's not impossible to "find yourself" and be true to yourself. When you're allowing yourself to open up and be yourself, you'll see such a huge shift in yourself, how you view yourself, and your connection with the people around you.

This is what I'm going to be focusing on throughout this section of the book. We're going to cover topics like becoming vulnerable, how to be yourself, learning about the art of giving and taking, and mastering how your words make such a big difference in other people's lives. Anyway, enough talking about—let's jump into it.

Method 9 – How to Open Up and Become Vulnerable

"When we were children, we used to think that when we were grown-up we would no longer be vulnerable. But to grow up is to accept vulnerability... To be alive is to be vulnerable." – Madeleine L'Engle

Brene Brown, a famous psychology researcher, author, and motivational speaker, speaks about how the most crucial aspect to think about when it comes to being happy and forming positive, meaningful, and fulfilling relationships with others comes down to being vulnerable. Being vulnerable, you may ask? Surely not.

When most people think of being vulnerable, they think it means to be weak or damaged. If I ask you to think about a "vulnerable animal," you'll probably think of a rescue animal before it's been rescued, or one that's been hurt and is being hunted by a predator on a nature documentary. Either way, it's not somewhere you consciously want to be.

But that's not entirely true.

When I, Brene Brown, or anybody else interested in happiness and social well-being talk about vulnerability, we're talking about the art of opening yourself up and being your true self, both with yourself and when you're around other people. Here's an example.

Let's say you're in a relationship with someone, and you have some trust issues. Your last partner cheated on you, and now you have these niggly little thoughts, doubts, and insecurities that come up now and then. They play on your mind and make you miserable, but you don't want to talk about them with your partner out of fear of being rejected. They might think you're silly or weak-minded, or even stupid for having these thoughts, so you keep them to yourself.

Anything that happens that triggers these feelings, you put up walls and push down insecurities, always trying not to think about them and never opening up and talking to other people, especially your partner, about them.

A situation like this never ends well. These insecurities build up and up over time, and eventually, they'll spill over the edge. You'll resent your partner because they keep triggering you, even though you won't know this at the time. Your paranoid attitude will cause you to do things like checking your partner's social media over and over or even reading through their text messages to see who they're talking to. We all do weird things in our relationships like this from time to time, but is it a healthy relationship? Of course not.

A healthy relationship would require you to be vulnerable and open up about your insecurities. This means being vulnerable and talking to your partner about how you feel and the stuff you're going through. Sure, they may try and help, or they may not know what to say, but that's not the point. The point is that you're opening up and allowing yourself to be out there and open to the world. You're saying this is me and what I'm going through, both good and bad, and I don't need to be ashamed of any of it.

Once you can get to this stage—and it's a journey, believe me—you'll find it's quite a liberating and refreshing experience. However, getting there is a whole other story, and it can definitely feel like a frightening one.

I know what you're thinking: *Uh, I don't want to open up about the things that are wrong with me and the things that scare me. I don't want to be open. I just want to push all the bad stuff down, never think about it, and put all those walls up to protect myself. If I don't think about it, it will go away eventually, right?*

Not so much. If you genuinely want to progress on your self-improvement journey and discover true happiness, even if this is just with yourself and not even concerning your relationships with other people, this is a process you're going to need to go through.

There's no denying that researchers like Brene Brown have pioneered this research field and put together all the science behind this over the last few decades. If you want to know more, I highly recommend checking out her book *Daring Greatly* or watching her TED talk, which is where it all started and remains one of the most-watched TED talks to this day. For now, though, I'll take some of the key lessons and takeaways that I learned from her speeches with you here.

The First Step is Courage

It would be amazing if you could ju
be vulnerable and open with every
focus on being yourself as naturall   .e, but
that would be too simple. Instead, the   .re some steps
to take.

However, the first point to think about is that being vulnerable, in the words of Brown herself, takes a certain amount of courage. You need to be brave, and there will come the point where you need to step out of your comfort zone and take the plunge. You could read every book and listen to every podcast on the subject, but there will always come a time where you open up to someone else and lay who you are out on the table for everyone else to see.

And this takes courage. You may not feel like you're ready now, but that's okay. You can build up to that over time. This is why it's wrong to see being vulnerable as a sign of weakness because, in fact, it's one of the strongest and most powerful things you can do. By going down this path and going for it, you'll be able to be your true and authentic self.

This will come in time, and you can start with little things to build up your courage like we've spoken about in previous chapters. I'm also not saying that you need out on the table to one person straight ...wouldn't go on a date and lay out all your ...ge on the first night. That's the best way to scare ...ople away because you're oversharing to someone you have no relationship with. It's all about building up your vulnerability and how open you can be with someone as your relationship with them grows.

The best thing to do is to take one thing at a time. Let's say you feel bad because you have a weight insecurity about yourself. You're talking to someone you're getting to know, and what they're saying is triggering you. Instead of pushing down your feelings and not speaking about it, you'll need to find the courage to open up and talk about how you feel. If someone is saying something like, "Oh, weight issues are just rubbish. It's just people trying to justify eating badly," you may want to share your beliefs on the subject.

You don't need to put someone down or take offense, but instead, just share your point of view. A lot of things happen here. Firstly, whether the person disagrees or not, they'll respect you for voicing your beliefs and not just going along with what they said. Then, they'll either listen to you, or they'll ignore you. If they listen and they're open to what you're saying and go along with something like "Oh yeah, I suppose I've never looked at it from this angle before," then this says a lot about that person, and they could be a good person to be friends with.

If, on the other hand, they say something like "Ppfft, what do you know?" and are pretty closed off about it, then do you want to have some kind of relationship with that person anyway? Probably not. Either way, it all starts with having the courage to open up and be yourself unapologetically.

Start Learning About Your True Self

I've spoken a lot about being your "true" self, or your authentic self, and you may be wondering who that is, and this in itself is an essential part of becoming vulnerable. But how can you be your true self if you don't know who that is?

For a lot of my life, I suffered from social anxiety, and as the years went by, I started to believe that this was who I was. I was the guy who worked in sales who went to work, went home, perhaps forced myself to see a friend every other now and then but couldn't wait to get home and just wrap myself up in my own world. I was single, a background guy, and just getting by. I used to write things like "I'm surviving, not thriving," quite regularly in my journal.

As I continued being this way, I started to believe that this was my identity. *How is there anything I can do about my social anxiety? It's just who I am at my very core.* It wasn't. Sure, you may be reading this and thinking, "Yeah, I am a shy, introverted person, and I get exhausted speaking to a lot of people." That's fine. What I'm saying is that so many have all these ideas in our heads about who we are, and the more often they're repeated, the more firmly we start to believe them. What we forget is that we're so much more than these identities that we accept for ourselves.

One of the most important aspects of becoming vulnerable is to become self-aware. This means understanding what beliefs you hold about yourself, how you identify with yourself, and therefore who you are. I could write a whole book in itself about this topic, so I'll leave you with the main takeaway.

Action Time – Become Vulnerable with Yourself

Start paying attention to your thoughts and emotions.

When anything happens in your life, whether you're watching the news, a movie, or chatting with someone, pay attention to how you feel and what emotions are coming up. When you get a moment, explore those emotions, discover how you feel, and then question why you feel this way. The answers you get may surprise you.

I remember I started doing this by beginning my own meditation practice and keeping a journal. I understand this is not for everyone, so figure out what works for you. Either way, I listened to my thoughts and feelings and realized that I wasn't a shy person who loved being alone. I was just lonely and justifying this loneliness. Understanding this opened the door for my self-care journey and gave me great insight into where I was in my life and who I am.

When you piece together all these points, you'll start learning about who you are, and you'll start being able to be yourself around other people. Yes, it takes a tremendous amount of courage to open up, but once you do, you'll be opening the door to some amazing relationships that you wouldn't even believe could exist.

Method 10 – Opening Your Door to the World

"Your real self may be hiding somewhere, look for it within, when you find yourself, you can freely be what you want to be." – Michael Bassey Johnson

Hand in hand with the last chapter, it's all well and good taking time to learn about yourself and who you are on the inside, but do you know who you are on the outside? One of the biggest problems for me while overcoming my social anxiety was that I had locked myself away in my apartment doing the bare minimum for so many years, it got to a point where I didn't know who I was.

What music and movies did I like? What food did I like? What kind of places did I want to travel to, and what types of books did I want to read? What activities, or exercises, or sports did I like doing? I indeed didn't have answers for these, and if asked, I would just go off the answers I would have given if I was still a teenager. Then, when I think about it, would those answers be the same? No, probably not.

As we change, our choices, tastes, likes, and dislikes change, and if you're looking to get to know someone and have a relationship with them, which is based on the foundations of common ground, then you need to know what you're interested in. This may sound like fundamental stuff, but I want you to take a moment to think about it.

Remember the music you used to like and how that's changed since you were a kid. And movies. Think about your guilty pleasures. All of these things become who you are, and they're not static things. You may hate musicals, and the very idea of them makes you cringe. Then, one day, you take the time to see one, perhaps not out of choice, and you enjoy yourself. Throughout an evening, something you had no interest in doesn't seem too bad. Your true self is continuously changing and evolving as you go through your life, but only if you let it.

I'm sure everyone would agree that it's easy to get stuck in your ways, especially as you get older and more experienced. Unless you're able to open your door to the world and embrace new experiences, even if you're giving them a try to see whether they're for you or not, this is how you grow as a person and understand yourself better. And of course, the better you understand yourself, the better your relationships will be because you won't be settling! See how it's all tying together?

It's true; there are going to be experiences out there that you don't like. That new sushi restaurant down the road? Yuck. I can't think of eating anything worse than raw fish, but then one day, you give it a go with a new friend, and lo and behold, you don't think it's too bad.

You even agree that you might consider going again. How about that?

Not only are you trying new experiences (which is a chance to connect with people in your life), but you're diving in and seeing who you are as a person, giving new things a go, and then making up your mind. What's more, science says that trying new things can be incredible for your brain and mindset.

Dr. Papp of Harvard University wrote:

"Until the mid-1990s, we thought that people were born with however many brain cells they would die with. We now know that the growth of new cells—a process called neurogenesis—occurs throughout life, even in older age,"

This means your brain is always growing new cells and is changing all the time. If you don't do new things and have new experiences, your brain doesn't tend to grow much because it's familiar with everything around it. Of course, not every day can be a new and wondrous adventure where you try new things, but you don't need to. Doing new things when you can is great for providing yourself with these benefits.

By stimulating your brain in different ways by doing new things and trying new activities, you're allowing your brain to grow in new and exciting ways. This will make you want to do more new things, and this is what it means to be outgoing. Remember how outgoing you were as a kid? It's entirely possible to get that back if you open your mind and say yes to new opportunities.

Action Time – Do Something New!

I bet you saw this one coming.

When I say do something new, you don't need to go for the most outlandish and crazy thing you can think of. I'm not saying go skydiving or take up wakeboarding, but if an opportunity presents itself, such as going to a new restaurant or seeing a play, joining a book club, or taking dance lessons, then this action time is to say yes.

Go into the activity with an open mind and give it your best shot. If you don't enjoy yourself, then that's fine. You're not going to enjoy everything, and you've still taken another step on your journey when it comes to understanding yourself. However, if you try something new and absolutely love it, you've opened a brand new door, of which there are plenty of beautiful new experiences for you to try.

Don't deny yourself of what could be something amazing!

You can try these new experiences with other people to improve your relationships, or you can take your experiences, and you'll have far more to talk about with everybody in your life. It all starts with you opening your mind to what could be.

Now that the last two chapters have included a bit of time working on yourself and your mindset, we're going to take a little trip back into the art of relationships themselves, this time taking a look at the art of giving and taking, or in this case, not taking.

Method 11 – Unconditionally Giving and Not Taking

"Blessed are those who can give without remembering, and take without forgetting" – Unknown

Method 3 was all about asking for favors and getting people to help you out as a way to spark a connection and implement trust, but one of the most fantastic ways to form and build on a friendship is by giving. And by giving, I mean giving and not just giving because you're expecting something back at a later date. In fact, I'm not even talking about the act of giving someone a gift or a physical item, but rather the art of reciprocating.

In 2009, a study was carried out by Peter DeSciolo and Robert Kurzban titled "The Alliance Hypothesis of Human Friendship." Within the study, the researchers discovered that if you want to have a "true friendship" with somebody, the age-old saying "I'll scratch your back and you scratch mine" might not cut the mustard. You need to go deeper than this.

When you think about it, the act of helping out someone else and them helping you out—aka, having each other's backs—makes sense. We've spoken a lot about the survival aspect of human nature, and how as social creatures, we're instinctively hardwired to come together to look out for one another. This, for many people, is the basis of most relationships, or at least a fundamental part. However, to take your relationship one step further, you'll need to learn to give without taking, which means to give without expecting anything in return.

Now, I know what you're thinking because I thought the same thing. If you give and give and give in relationships, then, of course, people are going to like you. You could always cover the bills for coffee, be a shoulder to cry on, organize everything, and always be the one carrying the conversations, but if you get nothing back ever, then this is just someone taking advantage of you, and that's true. Relationships are a balance between giving and taking, and there is a line that can be crossed. Don't worry; if you feel like this is the case in any of your relationships, you will have some deep-rooted feeling telling you that this is the case.

It will be very hard to miss.

The trick is to give in your relationships without losing sight of who you are, and without, as the Tiny Buddha website writes, sacrificing your needs. Doing this properly is a balancing act between being yourself and managing your own life, and then making a life with someone else. Of course, I'm not just talking about romantic and dating partners. This is evident in all kinds of relationships.

What I Mean By Giving

I'm writing this short section just so we're on the same page. When I say you're giving without taking, this can refer to anything. You may get home early from work and decide to deep clean the entire house before your partner gets home. You may get takeout to eat that night after someone in your life has had a stressful day. You may rub their feet in the evening or make them breakfast in bed off the cuff and for no real reason.

You may help them out by buying something when they're short on money or take them out just because you care about them. If they're going through a hard time, you might have them stay over, or you stay over at their house, you might do an activity to take their mind off things, or you may sit and talk about their situation with them.

It doesn't matter what you're giving; the point is that you're doing it because you want to make the other person happy, not because you want something in return. I had a friend in college who moved in with his girlfriend during his final year, and while an average guy, he had some weird ways of being in a relationship.

I remember once, while his girlfriend was doing her finals, that he tidied up the entire apartment, made dinner, and set up the lounge all nice for a movie night so his girlfriend could have a night off and destress. On the surface, this is a nice, selfless thing to do, and it's easy to see when you're doing things like this that relationships are strengthened by the minute.

However, the two ended up arguing, and the night was ruined. When my friend told me about this the next day, he explained how they got to bed after the movie, and he wanted to be intimate with his girlfriend. She said she was tired and wanted to go to sleep, but was grateful for the evening. He then got upset because he had put so much effort in and thought his girlfriend wasn't giving anything back. He thought her selfish.

Now, I agree with you if you think this is a very toxic way to look at things, but there's no doubt this is a trap that we all fall into every now and then. Just because we're doing something nice for someone, that doesn't mean that they have to do anything back. When you give without asking, it's unconditional. If the guy I went to college with had understood this, he would have gone to sleep with his girlfriend, finished a lovely evening, and the argument may never have happened.

Fast forward to the future. If he was having a stressful time, she might think to do something nice for him. Even if she doesn't, the relationship is still strong because you know that even if you're in a bad, stressful place, your friend or partner or whoever it is will be there to make you feel okay again.

In this situation, him acting up because he didn't get anything back taints the act of giving. Anything he does in the future, his girlfriend will think, *Oh well, he's only being nice because he wants something in return later,* and this way of thinking will help cause relationships to fall apart. The relationship becomes about a power balance, with people counting who owes who what, rather than just enjoying being in each other's company.

The Importance of Boundaries

I've said already that it's a fine line between giving to build a relationship and making someone happy and being used, but this is something you'll have to figure out for yourself. Say the guy is a decent guy who likes doing things to make his girlfriend happy. He organizes dates, cooks dinner, and sets up romantic evenings, which goes for months, perhaps even years.

However, while expecting nothing back, the relationship feels empty. She goes out with her friends all the time, and they spend very little time together outside of the things he organized. They lack a connection and don't do activities together, and the whole relationship feels very one-sided.

This can be a danger zone. In some cases, the guy may try extra hard to be nice in an attempt to make his girlfriend notice and appreciate him more, but then we're back at square one of him doing these things because he wants something in return. In this example, he wants her love and affection.

Unfortunately, there are no hard and fast guidelines to what you should do here, and it's up to you to decide where you put your boundaries. This is why it's essential to know and understand yourself.

A healthy relationship is like a dance. You step left, and you step right together. Sometimes one of you leads, and then you switch. You take it in turns to spin. Sure, there will be times when you stand on each other's toes, and you need to find your footing and rhythm again, and that's okay. However, if you're always trying to sync up or feel as though you're carrying all the weight, this isn't a healthy relationship.

Again, where you set your boundaries is up to you. If you feel like you're giving loads, but the relationships you're in are very one-sided, then talk to the person involved about how you feel. Have a conversation with yourself about how you feel and why you feel the way you do.

This can become a very complicated area when you dive into giving and taking. If you're giving because you want something back, whether it's a physical or emotional "thing," then this may be a sign you feel lonely or invalidated, and you're craving validation from someone else. This can be a form of attachment or a display of insecurity, which you'll want to work through by reading or getting counseling. This affects both professional and personal relationships of all kinds. Find the balance between giving because you care about the person and giving because you want something back.

If you're able to find the balance that works for you, and you've discovered your own boundaries, your relationships will begin to flourish. This is because you'll be taking care of your own needs for security and validation within yourself, and then everything you give to the people in your life comes from a place of love.

Action Time – Learn to Validate Yourself

A lot of giving happens in today's world because people want something back. As a kid, I would tidy the house and put all my toys away before my parents got home from work, not because I wanted to live in a tidy house and loved having space, but because I wanted my parents to tell me I did a good job. This is clearly not a healthy mindset to have because it leads to unhealthy giving.

For this action time, I want you to think about things you do in your life for other people and then ask yourself why you do them.

Sure, there are things in life that we just have to do, like washing the dishes or sweeping the floors, but pay attention to your thoughts when you do certain things. Are you buying your partner a coffee because you want them to forgive you for a mistaken comment, or because you just want a pleasant experience with them? Are you working hard on your project at work because you want to do well in your job or because you want to make your boss happy?

During my time in sales, a lot of my work was focused on making my boss happy, and it made me resent what

I did. Sure, the aim of the game is to make the customer happy and get good results, but I wasn't working to my standards (you could say my boundaries), but I was seeking out the validation of my boss.

When I switched my mindset to working as hard as I could to get a project done to the best of my ability, and I looked at it and thought, *Yes, this is exactly what I'm aiming for,* success came to me in ways I could never have imagined beforehand. When you're going throughout your life, start doing things for yourself, and validating yourself. Tell yourself you've done a job well, and treat yourself with the kindness you'd want from others.

From here, you'll find your boundaries naturally. You'll be able to give unconditionally to the people around you, especially to the ones you love, which can strengthen your relationship beyond belief. It takes practice, but it's a lifelong skill that will change everything.

Method 12 – Words: The Power of Light and Dark Magic

"Speak with integrity. Say only what you mean. Avoid using the word to speak against yourself or to gossip about others. Use your power of your word in the direction of truth and love." – Don Miguel Ruiz

One of the best books I've ever read is a book called *The Four Agreements* by Don Miguel Quiz. The book outlines four Toltec beliefs on how we live our lives and how our mind works. By understanding these beliefs, we can then choose how we want to show up in the world, all while choosing the kind of person we want to be and removing any self-limiting beliefs we may have.

One of the most powerful chapters in this book is about the words we use, which Don refers to as light and dark magic. Don writes amazingly, so I'm going to paraphrase the example he uses in the book about how the way we talk to people affects not only those individuals on a personal level but also our relationships with them. Using only words, you can pick someone up and place them on top of a mountain, or you can crush them. It's up to you.

The Story of the Singing Girl

In the chapter "The First Agreement," Don writes about a woman, a fairly normal, intelligent, kindhearted woman, and her daughter, who she loved a great deal. The mother gets home from work one day and, after a stressful day in the office through no fault of her own, she's in a bad mood.

When she arrives home, her daughter, who may be five or six, is singing. Her daughter loves to sing because it makes her feel free and beautiful, and it is her favorite thing to do. Stressed from the day and suffering from a giant headache, her mother gets home and says, "Can you please shut up? Your voice is doing my head in," or words to this effect.

Now, the mother didn't mean to be so aggressive. She was just acting out in the moment because she was suffering, and the daughter didn't mean to antagonize the mother; she didn't even know the mother was suffering. But, the mother's words cut into the daughter, and she then believed that her voice was horrible and was "doing her mother's head in." She believed her mother's words and never sang again, depriving herself of all those lovely, beautiful feelings and robbing the world of the beautiful gift she held.

Your words have power. Your words affect your relationships with others, and by understanding the power that your words have, you can choose how you can affect people with them. As Don eloquently puts it, will you use your words (magic) to cast spells of light or to create darkness in others? I think it goes without saying that relationships will thrive if you use your words to create light.

The Psychology of Words and the Mind

There is an absolute ton of research that's been done into the way words affect the brain that could easily fill several books, so I'll give you the lowdown.

First, the way you use your words affects how they are taken. Obviously. The tone, pitch, and intonation of the way you say something can mean you're happy, sad, passive-aggressive, sarcastic, etc. It all depends on how you present what you say. One study researching the impact of intelligible speech through the left temporal lobe found that the way we speak affects everyone on an incredibly deep, emotional level.

The example Learning Mind gives is if an everyday person said: "I have a dream" and compared that to how Martin Luther King said those famous four words, you have a very different emotional reaction because of how he said it and the emotion in his voice was sending such a powerful message through the words.

What's more, other researchers discovered that the type of language you use is incredibly reflective of how you see yourself and others around you. Dr. James Pennebaker from the University of Texas said:

"The way that people refer to themselves and others is highly diagnostic of their mental state."

This means that the language you use creates an image of you and the situation you're in. If you use negative or depressive language, this reflects how you feel, the same as if you use positive, energetic language.

Here are some statements you could say when someone asks how your day has been:

"It's been really good, thank you."

"It's been steady."

"It was okay."

"It was a day."

"Man, it was so good!"

Even through writing, you can tell what kind of day it was, even though from a linguistic point of view, they're all pretty close to each other on the "good day" scale, if that's even a thing.

Putting both these points together—what you say and how you say things—greatly impacts how people look at you and acknowledge you as an individual. If you want to be more charismatic, work on what you say and how you say it. If you want more in-depth relationships, work on what you say and how you say it. Let's put it into action.

Action Time – Using Words for Better Relationships

In any future conversion you have, I want you to slow down your responses and take a moment to think before you speak. Ah yes, that old chestnut of a saying. Do this both in the way you talk to others and, more importantly, the way you speak to yourself.

For example, when you go to work and you "have to" work on that latest project, you say this to a colleague, and it gives the impression you're forced to do something, you're complaining, or resisting reality. It's a bit of a moan, and doing this too often isn't going to win you any friends.

Instead, you could say something like, "I get to work on that new project." This portrays excitement in what you're doing, and even though you're only working, it creates a whole new impression of how you're looking at work and how others see you doing work. Everyone wants to have the kind of excitement you have for what they do, so in a sense, you're going to be inspiring them to do so.

The proof is in the pudding, so give it a try and see the results for yourself.

And that brings us nicely to the end of Part Three, or if I'm choosing my words carefully, it brings us to the start of Part Four. Part Four is my favorite part of this book because we're going to dive into the mechanics of what this book is about. Still focusing on you, I'm going to cover real actionable tips on being more charismatic, more confident, and more outgoing.

If you take anything away from this book and plan to use any methods, these are the methods you're going to want to focus on, but combining them with the other techniques in this book will work wonders. Well, what are you waiting for? Let's not hang around.

Part Four – It's Time to Work on You

While life would be fantastic if it worked this way, you can't snap your fingers and just decide to be more charismatic and confident. You can from a mental and psychological standpoint, but taking action to be more confident takes time and practice, just like anything else in life.

What I would recommend for this part of the book is to read through it and let the information settle, and then start practicing a bit at a time. Some aspects will resonate more with you than others. Some bits you might do already, and some bits you may never have thought of, so take the bits you want and work with them. If you're feeling spicy, then sure, try a bit you may not have thought about trying.

My point is, try things out and find what works for you. This way, you'll be discovering yourself and your style of charisma along the way. Let's go!

Method 13 – Becoming More Charismatic

"Charisma is the fragrance of soul." – Toba Beta

One of this book's main focuses was to help you understand what it takes to be more charismatic within yourself and your relationships. While you already know a lot of methods, this chapter is all about the hard and fast things you can do to actively become a more charismatic person. So firstly, what do I mean by "charisma?"

To be charismatic means to have the charm and attractiveness about you, both physically and intellectually, that makes other people want to be around you and want to know more about you. You may draw people in with how you talk and the way you are, you may have people hanging off your every word, or you may inspire something in people that make them want to be better.

I'm sure you know some charismatic people in your life, the kinds of people who make you feel like you want to be them, but not in an egotistical way—more in a natural way that just gives you a certain sense of peace around them. Fortunately, anyone can be this kind of person. It's something you learn and practice, although it does come more naturally to some people.

Here's how. By the way, these are all action times in their own right!

Awareness of Your Values

It's impossible to be confident and charismatic in yourself if you're unsure of what you stand for. This means you need to understand your values and what your abilities are. What do you stand for, what do you believe in, and what potential do you have to do amazing things in your life?

The answer to the last one is an unbelievably huge amount.

If you put your mind to something, you can achieve great things, but unless you truly believe you're capable of doing these things, then you're never going to be able to do them. Without this belief, it's impossible to be charismatic because you will believe that what you can do has limitations. Of course, you do have limitations, but being aware of what these are is essential because you can be confident and still have the ability to admit that there are things you can't do.

Own Integrity

Integrity is the ability to stick to your values and do the things you say you're going to do. This is essential when it comes to trusting relationships and with others around you and believing in yourself. For example, if you say you're going vegan and continue to eat meat, what you said is your values don't align with your actions. Therefore, you lose integrity in other people's eyes.

The bottom line of this point is to not do things that oppose your values. Of course, your values are allowed to change over time, especially as you gain a greater understanding of the world through others and your experiences, but you don't want to be corrupted by others.

Say you have the values of keeping your head clear and not smoking because it's unhealthy, but you go to a bar, and someone offers you a cigarette, and you give in to temptation or peer pressure. This means you lack integrity because you're not standing up for what you believe in, and this isn't a very charismatic way to be.

Think for Yourself

You've probably heard the phrase "to be a sheep," which means to follow everyone else around and just believe what you're told. This isn't a very charismatic way to be because you're not thinking for yourself and making up your own mind. The most charismatic people think for themselves, regardless of what the status quo thinks, which makes them such inspiring people to be around.

The best way to do this is not to take everything at face value but instead, dig a bit deeper. I had a conversation not too long ago with a man who worked in a factory his whole life and complained about how health and safety requirements have gotten out of control. I said I could see his point, but if he had lost a family member because of poor health and safety standards in a workplace, he would probably see things differently.

The sheep way to think is to go along with everything, perhaps the common opinion of the people around you. In contrast, a charismatic person will take the time to look at things from different angles before making up their minds and perspectives. What's more, a charismatic person can change their mind fluidly and won't be stuck in a singular way of thinking. This, in itself, is a very attractive quality to have.

Have a Flame Inside You

There is nothing more attractive than having a flame or a spark inside you that makes you go out and get what you want in the world. When I first decided I wanted to start writing books, it took me so long to get off the ground. I would toss and turn, write up drafts and then abandon them for months on end, thinking that I wasn't good enough and it wasn't going to work.

Is this an attractive and inspiring way to be? Obviously not.

Over time, after I had been working on my charisma and confidence, this began to light a fire in me, a burning passion for writing, and once I acknowledged that fire inside me, I knew there was nothing that was going to stop me from doing the things I wanted to do. The most charismatic people find this fire within themselves and stop at nothing to keep going. It's this energy that people are attracted to.

When it comes to your own life, ask yourself questions about what makes you feel good and passionate about life. What things in life make you feel alive? These aren't answers you're going to get overnight, or you may already have some idea, so find these things and pursue them. There's nothing more attractive or charismatic than a person with ambition and drive to make the most out of life.

Step Out of Your Comfort Zone

Charismatic people are comfortable with getting uncomfortable. There will always be times and situations throughout your life where you're uncomfortable and not feeling yourself, but how you respond and act in these situations will define you as an individual. Do you shy away from these situations and avoid them at all costs, or do you courageously face them and do everything you can to make the most out of them?

The choice is up to you.

Putting yourself in or simply accepting uncomfortable situations, rather than running from them, basically forces you to expand your comfort zone. This will help you grow as an individual, rather than remaining stagnant and where you are. This means you'll be open to new opportunities, thus becoming more outgoing and then being more naturally charismatic.

I still suffer from social anxiety from time to time, and there are definitely days where I'd love to stay in and watch Netflix. When I get invited to go out somewhere with a friend, it would be so easy to say no and just carry on with doing nothing. However, I recognize this mindset and will instead say yes, forcing myself to go to the event.

I always find this is the right decision and will buzz off the connection I receive from other people, meaning I can become more energetic and more confident in myself and have the opportunity to create new relationships. To cut a long story short, push your boundaries and limits, do things you don't want to do, and make the most out of any situation.

Be in Control of Your Emotions

Being an emotional person is not a great place to be. Now, I don't say this because emotions are bad. Emotions are useful because they're a clear indication of who we are as individuals and what we care about. However, if you allow your emotions to consume you and take over, this is where things can get problematic.

It's like when you're driving, and someone cuts you off or messes up, and you get this momentary rage ripple through you. You have a choice whether you let that emotion take control of you and ruin your day, or you choose to let it go and not bother you. This requires you to be mindful of your emotions and how you're feeling, and then choosing to react in the way you want to react, rather than just reacting and acting through the emotion itself.

If you're a slave to your emotions and let them control you, then you're not in control of your life. If you feel sad and act and talk to people through this filter of sadness, you're not yourself, and this is where problems occur. If you have an emotional conversation with a partner, say during an argument, this can lead you to say things you don't mean, leading to more problems and many regrets.

To be charismatic is to be more stable and in control of your emotions. Instead of letting them use you like a puppet, you are mindful of them and act with awareness of how you feel. This allows you to become a lot more grounded and rational with everything that happens in your life, and it's is an admirable trait to have.

If you follow these points and work on them where you can, you'll notice a considerable change in your sense of self, as you'll become far more charismatic and confident in yourself. You'll also notice that people will become drawn to you, attracted to you, and want to form relationships with you. You'll also feel far more fulfilled in yourself, which will do wonders for your satisfaction in life.

While many people use charisma and confidence interchangeably, and they are relatively similar, I'm going to dedicate the next chapter to solely improving your confidence and understanding the key differences between the two.

Method 14 – Everything You Need to Know about Confidence

"It is confidence in our bodies, minds, and spirits that allows us to keep looking for new adventures." – Oprah Winfrey

Just like the previous chapter, and so we're on the same page as we make our way through this one, the official definition of being confident is having the willingness to act accordingly when meeting life's challenges and having the drive to succeed. This goes hand in hand with stepping outside of your comfort zone, settling into uncomfortable situations, and even going on a journey to becoming more charismatic while believing in yourself.

If you don't have confidence, you're not going to have what it takes to be the best version of yourself. You need that passion and inner motivation to step forward into your true self and be yourself. Your relationship with yourself requires this, and this ripples out to every other relationship you'll have in your life, like all the ones we've spoken about in previous chapters.

Just like before, all of the following sections of this chapter are actionable, so there's no action time here. Just go through each point, see what resonates with you, and find what works for you. Take these points and guidelines that will help you to become the most confident version of yourself.

Find Your Limiting Beliefs

There will be times in your life where you are naturally confident already, so a great place to start when trying to expand this confidence "zone" is to take some time to think about where you are not so confident. Are you not so outspoken around strangers? Do you shy into yourself when you're around your parents? Do you feel overshadowed at work? Whenever you're trying to get better at anything in life, you need to know where you're starting from, and that's precisely what you're doing here.

Literally, sit down and make a list of when you get shy and unconfident in your life—making this list alone should be enough to highlight what areas of yourself you'll want to work on. From your list, make another, more condensed list of what areas of your life you want to be more confident in, and then start working on them!

Define Your Confidence Style

Everybody is confident in their own individual and personal way, and while being loud and outspoken may be ideal for some people, others take a quieter, more humble approach. For you, you may sit at either end of the scale or somewhere in the middle, so figure it out, and then you'll know what to aim for.

The best way to do this is to think about the times in your life when you felt the most confidence. Where were you, and what were you doing? Who were you with? When you can figure out why you felt so empowered during those moments, you'll have the opportunity to bring these ideas into other areas of your life.

Minimize Comparison With Others

Elon Musk once quoted that "comparison is the thief of joy," which is so true it hurts. Everybody is different and is walking their own path in life. Comparing yourself to someone else and what position they're in is only going to make you feel bad about yourself and diminish your achievements. The only person you should be comparing yourself with is yourself.

Let's say you're about to give a presentation at work, but you're comparing yourself with some of the best TED talk speakers in the world. Of course, your presentation will pale compared to these experienced speakers, but that doesn't mean you're bad or not worthy. Always aim to do the best you can and understand that you'll always get better through experience. Compare yourself to yourself rather than outwards to anyone else, and you'll find yourself growing in confidence with everything you do.

Keep on Learning

If you close your mind off to new ways of learning, you'll become stagnant, like a flowing river that ceases to flow and turns into a murky pool of water. When you take time to learn something new, whether it's a fact about the world or specifically a new skill, you'll give yourself a little boost in confidence because you're proving to yourself that you're enough and you're fully capable.

Always be open to learning new things, and you'll be amazed at what this can do for your mindset and how much of a boost it will give to your self-esteem.

Be True to Yourself

Yes, we're back to this point again, but I can't help but want to drive home how important this point is. Suppose you're masking yourself and pretending to be someone you're not for the supposed benefits of others. In that case, you're not going to be confident in yourself because you're spending all your energy focusing on hiding this person.

When you can freely be yourself and truly embrace who you are, there's no reason to spend energy on hiding yourself. A great way to do this is to think about who you are, then write down who you are and what makes you who you are. This relates to the previous chapter, where we spoke about understanding yourself and your values and then having the integrity to stick with these.

When you're true to yourself and reflect this to the people around you, you'll be able to be your genuine, confident self where you'll have nothing to hide from anyone. This naturally invites new opportunities for relationships because people know who you are and genuinely relate to you.

And with that, we come to the end of this method. Becoming confident using the methods above will take some time and practice, much like the rest of this book, but if you start implementing a few things at first, you'll start to see significant changes right off the bat. Just take the time to snowball these results and keep up the momentum of progress!

While we're on the subject of confidence, I did want to take a chapter to talk about outside appearances. We've spoken a lot about working on your inner self and discovering who you are so you can share this individual with other people and form amazing relationships, but what's on the outside does count for a lot as well. Allow me to explain.

Method 15 – Your Outside Reflects Your Inside

"To love oneself is the beginning of a lifelong romance. " – Oscar Wilde

Back in 2019, a study published in the *International Journal of Environmental Research and Public Health* discovered two things. One, poor hygiene habits are a prominent risk factor when it comes to preventable diseases. And secondly, poor hygiene is a risk factor when it comes to social rejection. And this makes sense.

I remember working a summer job in a factory during my second college year, and there was a guy there. He must have been 30-odd, and his breath was awful. And I'm not talking about the kind of breath where he may have eaten something, and it's stuck in his teeth that morning. I'm talking about consistent bad breath that seemed to get worse every day. He was a nightmare to work with at the time, but his poor hygiene habits only made things worse.

Put yourself in this situation. If you're at work or in a bar—any social situation—and you're talking to someone with nasty body odor, are you going to be focusing on what the person is saying, or are you going to be trying to get away from them? Probably the latter.

Likewise, if you see someone walking down the street and they're wearing dirty clothes and don't look like they look after themselves, do you want to associate yourself with this person? Turning the tables, if you're the person who looks like they don't look after themselves, do you think people will want to associate with you?

It's all well and good being a good, genuine person, but if you don't look after yourself, you're going to be pushing people away. More realistically, if you're not looking after yourself, you're probably not going to be confident in yourself, which will lead to you being even more socially anxious than you already are, which will ultimately make relationships harder to form and maintain.

To cut a long story short, it pays to look after yourself and to treat your body with respect, both for the attraction of others and for boosting the confidence you have in yourself. If you look and feel the part of the person you want to be, everything else will fall into place naturally. In this chapter, we're going to look at some of the things you can do to properly look after yourself.

Find Your Style

Everybody has their own style, so it's important for your confidence and self-esteem to find yours. What kind of clothes do you like to wear, and what clothes do you feel best in? It's good to try different clothes to see what you like and don't like, and don't just stick with what you know because it's what you've always liked.

During the peak years of my social anxiety, I would only wear tracksuit bottoms and hoodies, always black, and pretty much nothing else. However, I pulled some old button-up shirts and started wearing them after reading up on how we should dress to be comfortable, not just for other people. The positive effects were instant. I felt so much better about myself, and even just choosing nice clothes for me to wear was boosting my self-confidence and making it feel as though I was putting effort into myself. This then started to ripple out into other areas of my life.

Even if you're not someone who's into fashion, taking the time to pick out and wear clothes that make you feel good can have such a positive effect on your confidence and self-esteem. If you're looking for a way to empower yourself, this is one of the best approaches to take.

Develop a Daily Routine

Proper hygiene is vital if you want to be confident in yourself, and if you want others to be attracted to you. I'm sure you've had examples in your own life where you've met someone with poor hygiene who made you want to be anywhere but next to them. Don't be that person!

The best way to stay on top of your hygiene efforts is to get yourself a daily and weekly routine. Your daily routine should consist of all the essentials like brushing your teeth twice a day for two minutes at a time, washing your skin thoroughly, both in the morning and at night, and making sure you wear fresh socks and underwear every day.

You can also develop a skincare routine if you're interested in using products to counter certain conditions, such as dry skin or acne. You should do other essential hygiene tips now and then, such as flossing, using mouthwash, and shaving or plucking eyebrows. It's really up to you what you do. It's just a case of actually putting effort into seeing what you can do and then sticking with it until it becomes a habit.

Even taking the time to learn how to brush your teeth properly can make a world of difference. I had an awful wisdom tooth experience that opened my eyes to how important dental care is. I bought an electric toothbrush that connects to an app that monitors where you're brushing your teeth and how much pressure you're putting on the brush. It works like a treat.

All of this combined means you're taking the time to look after yourself, thus helping you love yourself more and making yourself incredibly attractive to the people around you.

Exercise Regularly

I know you probably saw this one coming, but again, it's an essential part of looking after yourself. If you can get it down to a routine where you don't even need to think about it, exercising regularly will give you so much more energy as you go through your day; you'll be fitter, healthier, happier, more satisfied with your life, and all of this is going to make you feel good about yourself and will attract other people if you're working out and looking your best.

Again, you don't need a vigorous exercise plan but rather need to take time to figure out what you want to do and how you can make exercising enjoyable. Do you like running, swimming, or jogging? Do you want to join a team? Would you rather go to a gym or exercise outside? Try all the options available to you to see which activity you resonate with, therefore narrowing down the activities you're more likely to stick with for more extended periods of time.

Endless studies prove that exercise is important for maintaining a balanced state of mental health, reducing stress levels, and building up your confidence. You'll also improve your social relationships when you exercise with a partner, friend, join a team, and improve your abilities to successfully create powerful and beneficial habits.

Eat a Healthy Diet

Eating a proper, healthy diet goes hand in hand with exercising properly and making sure you're looking after yourself in the best possible way, therefore allowing all the positive benefits to come into your life. Now, this isn't a traditional diet point, and I'm not going to harp on about how you should cut out a load of foods and be strict via creating meal plans and punishing yourself if you get takeout. Sure, you can be strict if that's what works for you, but if you're an average person, then here are some tips that take minimal effort.

First, increase the amount of fruit and veggies you eat. You should typically be aiming for five full portions a day, which roughly translates into 80-gram portions. That's 80 grams of grapes, or an apple, or a large banana, for example. You can eat veggies any way you want, whether that's frozen, fresh, dried, or even juiced, which is great when you don't want to spend a fortune on food. You can simply shop in the best way to suit you.

Secondly, try to avoid snacking. Eat three set meals per day, making sure not to skip breakfast, and minimize eating between these meals. Obviously, you can if you're hungry, but having three meals per day at set times helps to set your body up in a rhythm and natural pattern, which will do it a world of good when it comes to digestion and giving your body the energy it needs to get through the day.

118

You could also try intermittent fasting. I would research this yourself because there are many options out there, but the best option that worked for me was only eating between the hours of 12 pm and 8 pm. This gives the body 16 hours to digest food and allows you to rest and digest properly.

On top of this, make sure you're not overeating sugar, fatty foods, and salt. The final consideration to think about is drinking enough water, of which you should be aiming for around two liters per day. Getting a one-liter bottle was one of the best purchases I made because you just need to fill it up twice a day, and you know you've drunk enough. The benefits from this water point alone will bring so much positive change into your life.

Now, I could go on and on about all the health tips you could follow, and I really could write a whole other book just about that topic, but fortunately, there is a ton of information online. Remember, before you make any drastic changes to your lifestyle, make sure you're taking things slow and speaking to a healthcare professional, especially if you're living with any kind of physical condition.

Bringing everything full circle, if you can look after yourself health-wise, then your confidence and self-esteem will go through the roof. You'll feel better about yourself, which will have a massive effect on your relationships, both new and old. You'll want to spend time with people, and they'll want to spend time with you. By following these tips, changes in your life will happen, so naturally, you'll be able to look back in a few months and find yourself amazed and everything that has happened.

Now, ready for the final characteristic you need to have to form healthy relationships?

Method 16 – Trust is Everything

"Trust takes years to build, seconds to break, and forever to repair." – Unknown

If you've ever been lied to or betrayed by someone, then you know how much it hurts to have trust in a relationship broken. Having trust is fundamental to any relationship. Even though you might see yourself as a trustworthy person, it's vital that you think about how you can be more trustworthy and prove this to the people around you consistently and naturally.

Take a moment to think about how often you tell little white lies. The lies that don't mean anything, but you tell them anyway. In sales, I used to say all the time that work on a project was done, and I'll send it over Monday because my internet was acting up. The work wasn't done. I was just sitting at home feeling sorry for myself and was making up excuses to give myself more time. Now, you might think these lies are harmless, but when people can see through them, they create an impression of you, and they damage your relationships.

From the other person's perspective, they see that you're going through a rough time but don't want to approach you. Obviously, you're lying because you don't want to talk about it. However, that person will feel negatively towards you because you lied to them, and while it may seem little, they're not going to trust you on much bigger, more important topics.

Imagine if, taking this example, you were to say to your boss, "I haven't been able to do the work because I've been struggling this week. I'm going to get it done by Monday for sure. I just need a little time to get myself back on track." Sure, there's probably a voice in your head telling you that wouldn't go down so well, but at least you were honest, and your boss is far more likely to respect you for saying this, thus improving your relationship with them. It's an incredibly respectful thing to do.

A 2016 global study on some of the top CEOs in the world found that 55% of CEOs in the world's biggest companies said that a "lack of trust" was among the biggest threats to a company's stability and success. Just like in my example above, if you don't trust the people you're working with, this creates a huge shift in the team's dynamic because nobody knows who is telling the truth. Problems are guaranteed to arise at some point.

The same applies to your relationships. If you break trust in a relationship, both romantic relationships or friendships, depending on the person involved, they may never fully trust you again, and there's no stability. It doesn't matter what you say to that other person; they can just say, "I don't believe you," and there's nothing you can do to make things better.

As a rule of thumb, always be honest with people from the moment you meet them. Never give them a reason to think you're untrustworthy. If people can trust you with their lives, your relationships will be stronger than you can imagine. So, how do you do it?

How to Be More Trustworthy in Your Relationships

Of course, I could just say for this point that you shouldn't tell lies, and this can be enough, but it's not. People all have different life experiences, and if you meet someone who's been lied to by the people in their lives for as long as they can remember, they may not trust you, even if you're a trustworthy person. You need to have the integrity to prove that you are, and you can do this by following the points below.

Start Off Slow and Build Up Trust

We already spoke about how important it is to be vulnerable, which comes up again here. To build trust, you need to be vulnerable. If you're openly and honestly telling people about how you think and feel, you're telling people that you're an open book and you can be trusted since you're trusting them with what you're telling them.

However, it's important to remember when you're getting to know someone that you don't just jump in the deep end and share all your baggage. This is known as being "too vulnerable," as we discussed before. Start slowly when you're getting to know someone and build up to the more intimate and vulnerable details of your thinking as you go. Remember, while you want the other person to trust you, you always want to be able to trust them, so find the right balance between giving and taking.

Putting in the Time

Imagine two people are working in an office together. They have worked in the same office for 30 years and only really talk in passing. They talk about the weather and exchange short statements about changes in the company. You wouldn't call them close or even friends, despite knowing each other for so long.

Now compare that to two people who work on projects together in the same office. They have been working together for two months, but work very close to each other, are interacting every single day about work and share their social lives, and have to experience both the good and the bad together where they work.

The relationship, while in similar circumstances physically, produces two very different relationships. Trust doesn't happen overnight, but it doesn't come without effort. If you want someone's trust, you need to put in the time and have experiences with this person. The more positive time you put in the relationship, the more you'll be trusted.

Avoid Emotionally Harming Someone

When someone tells you something that they're trusting you with, you must pay them respect and avoid damaging them and hurting them, even if you do it unintentionally. This is one of the quickest ways to break your trust with someone.

Let's say someone is telling you something about their private life that they've been a bit unsure about telling anyone else. Perhaps it's private, or maybe they think that nobody else cares. The worst thing you can do is belittle that person, make them feel less than normal, or even view them with contempt, disgust, or condescend to them. The more intimate your relationship is with someone, the more important it is not to cross a line because your words will be more powerful, the closer you are to someone.

Remember, your words have the ability to create magic, and it's up to you what spells you cast.

This doesn't mean you can't be honest about how you feel with the people in your life and that you have to effectively shut up and listen. It means you need to be mindful of the way you're reacting to something. If someone tells you about their partner, remember that you're only hearing one side of the story, an emotionally tainted side at that, and therefore you shouldn't judge or jump to conclusions.

In many cases, unless someone asks for advice, you don't need to give it, and the person is instead speaking to you because they just want to get something off of their chest. A great way to deal with this point is simply, no matter what the situation is, to respect them and give them the benefit of the doubt until proven otherwise. This way, you can maintain your connection and your trust no matter what.

Be Honest with Your Feelings

Just like the example at the beginning of this chapter when you could be talking to your boss when you're not feeling yourself, you must remain true to yourself and others around you, especially when it's hard and tough to do so. Sometimes, telling the truth can seem like a hard thing to do, and you may be afraid of hurting others, letting them down, or even putting yourself in a bad light.

However, the best relationships are formed between people who can be open and honest, even if it would be easier not to. This will create a huge amount of respect for you among the people in your relationships, and the trust will only help strengthen these connections.

With all these points in the chapters we've covered throughout this part of the book, you should have more than enough information to work with. When it comes to working on yourself, I want to remind you not to try and change everything at once, nor should you try and believe that you need changing.

You are perfectly enough for the world just the way you are right now, and this is a mantra you should repeat for a considerable boost in your self-confidence! However, no matter how you look at it, everything in life is a skill, and skills can be practiced. All the points we've covered are backed by science to deliver positive results into your life. These will help make you happier, more fulfilled, and healthier in general, and all of these effects will be seen throughout your relationships.

Part Five – Maintaining Your Relationships & Looking to the Future

And here we are, Part Five. Throughout this book, we've covered everything you'll want to know when it comes to increasing your charisma, building your confidence, winning friends, making people attracted to you, and developing all your relationships from your professional connections to your romantic partners and everyone in between and on either side.

Within this final chapter, I'm going to be leaving you with three methods you'll want to bear in mind for the future of your self-development journey. These are how you spend your time with people and develop patience with yourself, others, and your entire journey through life, and how to forgive.

Method 17 – Time: Quality Over Quantity

"Relationships are built on small, consistent deposits of time. You can't cram for what's most important. If you want to connect with your kids, you've got to be available consistently, not randomly." – Andy Stanley

When I was a teenager, I found myself in some very clingy relationships. I had maybe two people I would call best friends and would jump from one romantic relationship to another and would spend all my time with these people. Now, I had a large group of friends but rarely spent time with them. For some crazy reason, I believed that I would spend all my time with the same people, and that's how life worked.

It doesn't work this way, and in fact, it's a very unhealthy way to live life.

Just because you love someone and have a connection with them doesn't mean you should spend all your time with them. The time you spend with people—anybody for that matter, not just the people who are close to you—should be quality time. Quality time could be a couple of hours once a week, or even every now and then. It all depends on the individual relationship.

It can be counterproductive to your relationship if you spend too much time with someone because you're not allowing each other to see other people, thus getting a fresh perspective on the work, and you do not have alone time to be by yourself, process emotions, and think your own thoughts free from distraction. We all need alone time now and then, even if we don't want to admit it.

A study published back in 1999 by Zimmer and Gembeck found that women who jump into new relationships and spend a lot of time with their partners will rapidly spend less time with their friends, and this creates problems in both the romantic relationship and the friendship.

If you're spending all your time with just a handful of people all the time, then any goals or aspirations you'll want to work on will be impossible because where are you going to find the time? You'll also be hindering the achievements of the people you're spending time with, and this can lead to both attachment and resentment. If you're resenting each other, even if you're not thinking it directly, this will again cause problems within the relationship.

So, the best thing to do here is to take a step back and find balance. Hand in hand with creating memories and having positive experiences with people, don't spend all your time with other people you're close to but remember to be an individual and live your own life. The other people in your relationships shouldn't be your entire life, but rather people that complement it and are a part of it.

Action Time – Have Some You Time

You're going to appreciate this action time because it feels so good and energizing when you've done it properly. Once a week, I want you to disconnect from the world for an hour or so. This means turning off your phone or at least blocking your social media apps. Watch a movie from start to finish, read a book, learn a language, meditate, have a bath, or do whatever you want to do, but do whatever it is as quality time with yourself.

Give yourself the same amount of attention and love you would give when spending time with someone you love. By doing this regularly, you'll be able to connect and stay connected with who you are as a person, and then you'll be able to bring this truly-loved self into your relationships.

Method 18 – Developing Patience for the Journey

"To lose patience is to lose the battle." – Mahatma Gandhi

Whether you're developing yourself, getting to know someone, dealing with a difficult time in your relationship, or basically dealing with any kind of situation in life, you're going to need patience. Focusing on the relationship side of things, if you don't have patience, you'll find that stressful situations start to snowball.

When something happens, or we take something personally, or the other person struggles to find the right words to say, you may find yourself becoming irritable, defensive, or even lashing out and saying something you don't mean. This will only make matters worse and cause more stress, and therefore more problems, and the vicious cycle continues.

Developing patience is all about feeling those initially stressful emotions, taking a deep breath, and then allowing yourself to remain grounded and calm. Let's say someone at work is freaking out because some part of the project hasn't been done, and the client is breathing down the boss's neck. Now everyone is getting stressed.

Instead of freaking out alongside everyone else and watching the team fall apart (some people getting thrown under the bus and people starting to point fingers), you remain patient and let everyone have their turn. When it comes to you, you instead speak from a calm place, highlight the work that needs to be done, and then what solutions are available. This will generate a huge amount of respect from the people around you.

If you go through life with an impatient attitude, then the only person who will suffer is you. Always take time to see things, even the worst situations, from a peaceful state of mind. This can, admittedly, feel impossible to do sometimes, especially when the people you're interacting with are showing no patience whatsoever. Still, it's always a good idea for your mental well-being to remain cool, calm, and collected.

Action Time – How to Develop Patience

There are endless ways to be more patient. You could meditate, journal, and even write affirmations on your hands to remind yourself to be more patient throughout the day. I tried setting alarms on my phone tagged with "be more patient" texts to remind me at random times.

However, the one key way to become more patient, and the act that worked for me was simply to breathe. I suppose this is a kind of meditation, but it didn't matter what I was doing or who I was with. I started working on the habit of taking a deep breath before doing or saying anything. I didn't make it super obvious, but it was more of a mindful breath. Even in favorable situations, like hanging out with friends, this was something I did.

This breath was a reminder to be patient. Eventually, when I found myself in a less-than-desirable situation, which I didn't have to wait long for, I would breathe and stay patient, meaning I was much more grounded when it came to answering other people and thinking with a sound state of mind. This process helped me to develop a much more positive mindset towards life and made my relationships stronger.

Method 19 – The Power of Forgiveness

"There is no love without forgiveness, and there is no forgiveness without love." – Bryant H. McGill

I've saved this point 'til now because I wanted to end with a bang. Before sitting down to write this book, I read about the story of Immaculee Llibagiza. In fact, it was her story that partly inspired me to write this book, simply because her story is so powerful and it shows how so many of us are missing out on such an important aspect of our relationships.

Every person on the planet is a human being and only a human being. It seems obvious, but so many of us forget that being human means we can make mistakes, and we're guaranteed to make many throughout our lives. We're going to hurt other people at some point, even when we try not to, and other people are going to hurt us. However, no matter what, learning about the power behind forgiveness can change everything.

I spoke briefly about being cheated on by my ex-girlfriend a few years ago and being so angry, I punched a windscreen, and this was hate and anger I held on to for years. I blamed my sadness and pain on my ex, and when I found myself getting involved in new relationships, I still held that resentment, and it affected me in so many ways. I had trust issues and was paranoid, and simply believed I was going to be hurt again. The problem wasn't with my new partners or friends; it was with me. I hadn't learned to let go of the past.

The Story of Immaculee Llibagiza

Immaculee Llibagiza was born in Uganda, and as a young girl, she was subject to the Ugandan genocide and traumatic event that ravaged the country. Being a girl, barely a teenager, Immaculee was hidden in a Catholic priest's bathroom in his house with a group of other girls while the militia came through to kill anyone who wasn't of the superior religion.

The bathroom was three feet by four feet. While the priest thought hiding the girls would be something he did for a few days until the militia moved on, the genocide lasted several months. Immaculee remained in that bathroom, cramped and surrounded by other girls for several months, never speaking a word to anyone the entire time out of fear of being discovered. The bathroom door was hidden behind a bookshelf to hide it while the house was raided multiple times.

Eventually, the government was overthrown and a new party elected. The men involved in the genocide were arrested, and the country taken back under control, but not before over one million people had been killed by the rampage. When Immaculee emerged from the bathroom, she discovered she had lost everyone. Her mother, her brothers, and friends. Everyone had been killed. Her small town had been destroyed.

Immaculee had spent her time in the bathroom, reading the Bible over and over again, praying to God that everyone was going to be okay, and it was here she learned about forgiveness. Years passed, and she was given the opportunity to see the man who killed her family, who was locked in prison.

When she arrived, the guard offered to hold the man so she could hit him and spit on him, and do whatever she wanted to take revenge on the man for killing all those people, just like other people had been doing when they visited for years. The man looked broken.

Instead, Immaculee did the unthinkable. She sat opposite the man, took his hand, and said, "I forgive you." Such an incredibly powerful moment.

The Power of Forgiving

Many of us will never be in a situation like Immaculee was, and reading her story, you may think about how much rage and hurt you would hold towards the man who killed everyone you know and brought such pain and suffering into your life. However, Immaculee knew that forgiving was healing, and holding so much pain and resentment towards the man would only bring more pain and suffering into her life.

She wanted to heal and let the pain go and find peace with the situation, which meant forgiving him for what he had done. It takes a certain kind of strength to do this, but I truly believe that Immaculee is on to something. By holding in everything that anyone has ever done to hurt you, you're only ever hurting yourself. Holding any pain or hurt will affect all your relationships, including your relationship with yourself.

Action Time – Forgive Someone

I'm not saying you need to reach out and actively forgive someone for something they've done in the past. It might be a little weird contacting someone you haven't spoken to for many years. What you can do, however, is write down some past resentment or hurt that you feel like you're still holding on to.

Write it down on a piece of paper with a message to the person who's involved. Write as much or as little as you want, vent out all your anger and feelings, and put all your thoughts down in a letter format. In the end, simply write, *I forgive you*. Read the letter through, then rip it up and throw it away or burn it; a statement that will help you let go and truly forgive.

Be mindful of how you feel the following days after doing this, and you'll see just how powerful it can be.

Final Thoughts

And with that, we come to the end of our journey!

I hope more than anything you were able to find value in these pages and that you enjoyed reading this book as much as I enjoyed writing it. Self-discovery and development of any kind can be scary and daunting, and very isolating if you're not sure where you're going or what you're doing, but I hope this book can act as a guide to help you find your way and make the improvements you want to make in your life.

Relationships are such an essential part of living, and so using the methods and information you've just read, it would be amazing to see how much of a difference they make. There's no end to the benefits that boosting your charisma and confidence can bring, and, as the saying goes, it's not what you know in life, but who you know, and know you've got the skills to bring these amazing relationships to life. Who knows what opportunities now await you.

I would always like to take this moment to ask that if you did enjoy this book, you could leave a review for me. I love hearing all the fantastic stories of how these words have inspired others, and it inspires me to write more! I look forward to hearing from you!

And with that, we must part ways. I wish you the best of luck on your journey to a brighter, happier, and more energized version of yourself. I just know if you put these methods into practice, you're going to experience such positive developments that will change your life!

See you soon!

References

Loneliness Statistics and Data | SocialPro. SocialPro. (2020). Retrieved 1 December 2020, from https://socialpronow.com/loneliness-statistics/#1.

Sonnby–Borgström, M., 2020. *Automatic Mimicry Reactions As Related To Differences In Emotional Empathy*.

When you smile, the world smiles at you: ERP evidence for self. Retrieved December 1, 2020, from https://academic.oup.com/scan/article/10/10/1316/1 646200

There's Magic in Your Smile | Psychology Today UK. Retrieved December 1, 2020, from https://www.psychologytoday.com/gb/blog/cutting-edge-leadership/201206/there-s-magic-in-your-smile

Why Do We Feel Lonely? - Big Think. Retrieved December 1, 2020, from https://bigthink.com/ideafeed/why-do-we-feel-lonely

Coaching Children in Social Skills for Friendship Making. Retrieved December 1, 2020, from https://www.jstor.org/stable/1128645

Social Connections and Happiness. Retrieved December 1, 2020, from https://www.theworldcounts.com/happiness/social-connections-and-happiness

Social support: Tap this tool to beat stress - Mayo Clinic. Retrieved December 1, 2020, from https://www.mayoclinic.org/healthy-lifestyle/stress-management/in-depth/social-support/art-20044445

Jecker, J., & Landy, D. (1969). Liking a Person as a Function of Doing Him a Favour. *Human Relations*, 22(4), 371-378. https://doi.org/10.1177/001872676902200407

Deep Listening in Personal Relationships | Psychology Today. Retrieved December 1, 2020, from https://www.psychologytoday.com/us/blog/the-empowerment-diary/201708/deep-listening-in-personal-relationships

Why Be Honest?. Psychology Today. (2020). Retrieved 1 December 2020, from https://www.psychologytoday.com/us/blog/happines s-in-world/201402/why-be-honest.

Worldometer - real time world statistics. Worldometer. (2020). Retrieved 1 December 2020, from https://www.worldometers.info/.

8 Easy Ways to Have Better Conversations - The Art of Charm. The Art of Charm. (2020). Retrieved 1 December 2020, from https://theartofcharm.com/art-of-business/networking/easy-ways-to-have-better-conversations/.

Human Brains Are Hardwired for Empathy, Friendship, Study Shows. UVA Today. (2020). Retrieved 1 December 2020, from https://news.virginia.edu/content/human-brains-are-hardwired-empathy-friendship-study-shows.

Kumashiro, M., & Sedikides, C. (2005). Taking on board liability-focused information: Close personal relationships as a self-bolstering resource. *Psychological Science, 16,* 732-739.

Oishi, S. (2010). The psychology of residential mobility: Implications for the self, social relationships, and well-being. *Perspectives on Psychological Science, 5,* 5-21.

Schnall, S., Harber, K. D., Stefanucci, J. K., & Proffitt, D. R. (2008). Social support and the perception of geographical slant. *Journal of Experimental Social Psychology, 44,* 1246-1255.

Low on Self-Control? Surrounding Yourself With Strong-Willed Friends May Help. Association for Psychological Science - APS. (2020). Retrieved 1 December 2020, from https://www.psychologicalscience.org/news/releases/low-on-self-control-surrounding-yourself-with-strong-willed-friends-may-help.html.

Partners in Crime: When Do Friends Conspire to Eat More Chocolate?. Press.uchicago.edu. (2020). Retrieved 1 December 2020, from https://press.uchicago.edu/pressReleases/2014/May /0522JCRlowe.html.

Friendology: The Science of Friendship. Psychology Today. (2020). Retrieved 1 December 2020, from https://www.psychologytoday.com/us/blog/lifetime-connections/201805/friendology-the-science-friendship.

Margarita Tartakovsky, M. (2020). *3 Keys to a Strong Relationship*. World of Psychology. Retrieved 1 December 2020, from https://psychcentral.com/blog/3-keys-to-a-strong-relationship/.

Hedrick, M. (2020). *What it Means to be Vulnerable*. World of Psychology. Retrieved 1 December 2020, from https://psychcentral.com/blog/what-it-means-to-be-vulnerable/.

What Does It Mean to Be Vulnerable? 13 Ways You Can Open Up More. LovePanky - Your Guide to Better Love and Relationships. (2020). Retrieved 1 December 2020, from https://www.lovepanky.com/my-life/better-life/what-does-it-mean-to-be-vulnerable.

5 Life-Altering Lessons from Brené Brown's The Power of Vulnerability. Retrieved December 1, 2020, from

https://www.goalcast.com/2018/06/18/5-lessons-brene-brown-the-power-of-vulnerability/

The power of vulnerability | Brené Brown - YouTube. Retrieved December 1, 2020, from https://www.youtube.com/watch?v=iCvmsMzlF7o

Rev up your thinking skills by trying something new - Harvard Health. Retrieved December 1, 2020, from https://www.health.harvard.edu/healthy-aging/rev-up-your-thinking-skills-by-trying-something-new

DeScioli, P., & Kurzban, R. (2009). The Alliance Hypothesis for Human Friendship. *PLoS ONE*, 4(6), e5802. https://doi.org/10.1371/journal.pone.0005802

Ruiz, M., & WIlton, N. (2004). *The Four Agreements*.

The Power and Psychology of Words on Our Minds - Learning Mind. Retrieved December 1, 2020, from https://www.learning-mind.com/the-power-and-psychology-of-words-on-our-minds/

The Power of Words: How to Affect Other People with Words. Retrieved December 1, 2020, from https://www.pyradyne.com/blogs/health-nutrition/the-power-of-words-how-to-affect-other-people-with-words

Scott, S. K. (2000). Identification of a pathway for intelligible speech in the left temporal lobe. *Brain*,

123(12), 2400-2406. https://doi.org/10.1093/brain/123.12.2400

Pennebaker, J. W., Mehl, M. R., & Niederhoffer, K. G. (2003). Psychological Aspects of Natural Language Use: Our Words, Our Selves. *Annual Review of Psychology*, 54(1), 547-577. https://doi.org/10.1146/annurev.psych.54.101601.145 041

How to Use the Power of Words to Transform Your Life - Learning. Retrieved December 1, 2020, from https://www.learning-mind.com/how-to-use-the-power-of-words/

To Feel Better About Yourself, Learn A Small New Skill. Retrieved December 1, 2020, from https://vitals.lifehacker.com/to-feel-better-about-yourself-learn-a-small-new-skill-1838530362

Ramos–Morcillo, Moreno–Martínez, Susarte, Hueso–Montoro, & Ruzafa–Martínez. (2019). Social Determinants of Health, the Family, and Children's Personal Hygiene: A Comparative Study. *International Journal of Environmental Research and Public Health*, 16(23), 4713. https://doi.org/10.3390/ijerph16234713

19th Annual Global CEO Survey: Redefining business success in a changing world. Retrieved December 1, 2020, from https://www.pwc.com/gx/en/ceo-survey/2016/landing-page/pwc-19th-annual-global-ceo-survey.pdf

The 3 Elements of Trust. Retrieved December 1, 2020, from https://hbr.org/2019/02/the-3-elements-of-trust

Effect of relationship experience on trust recovery following a breach. Retrieved December 1, 2020, from https://www.pnas.org/content/110/38/15236

How We Understand Trust in Romantic Relationships: Key Findings. Retrieved December 1, 2020, from https://www.kellogg.northwestern.edu/trust-project/videos/finkel-how-we-understand-trust-in-romantic-relationships-key-findings.aspx

7 Ways to Build Trust in a Relationship | Psychology Today. Retrieved December 1, 2020, from https://www.psychologytoday.com/us/blog/friendship-20/201812/7-ways-build-trust-in-relationship

How Much Time Should Couples Spend Together? | Psychology. Retrieved December 1, 2020, from https://www.psychologytoday.com/us/blog/meet-catch-and-keep/201406/how-much-time-should-couples-spend-together

Importance of Patience in Life. Retrieved December 1, 2020, from https://www.wisdomtimes.com/blog/importance-of-patience-in-life/

Rwandan genocide survivor shares story of forgiveness | Angelus. Retrieved December 1, 2020, from https://angelusnews.com/local/la-catholics/rwandan-genocide-survivor-shares-story-of-forgiveness/

Printed in Great Britain
by Amazon

56928508R00092